ACADEMY OF POWERFUL CAREGIVERS

Module 1: Motivation of a Caregiver

I0170073

by Kevin W. Shorter

https://JosiahsCovenant.com/

https://Prayer-Coach.com/

Dedications

I dedicate this book to work my wife and I started in China, Josiah's Covenant. It is my desire for the success of this work that led me to create this curriculum.

Allison, Rachel, Elizabeth, and I have invested so much into creating family for teenage orphan girls, giving them a place to land after the orphanage and protecting them from human trafficking. This work has stolen our time but also given us experiences with God that we would never regret.

I also want to include David and Phoebe. You both have believed in the vision of Josiah's Covenant and sacrificed yourselves for its success. Our family loves you very much.

Finally, I want to thank our financial supporters and prayer partners of Josiah's Covenant who have made it possible for us to go.

Table of Contents

4

1

How to Give Lasting Help

I'm glad you made the decision to join us for this journey into the first module of the Academy of Powerful Caregivers: The Motivation of a Caregiver. During this module, you will gain an understanding of the source that drives caregivers for the long-term and gain tools to help you give without burning out. By looking at the motivation you have to give to others, we will help maintain your alignment to those things that will keep you thriving for the long run.

The purpose of this academy is to create a culture of caregivers who can sit with people in their pain and help lead them to lasting help. My wife and I have started a non-profit to care for teenage orphan girls in China and these lessons were intended to create structure for our growth. As we began building our organization, we knew we needed something in place to cultivate the right culture for the work we want to accomplish. We feel these lessons are also beneficial for the larger Christian community.

It Takes More Than A Noble Desire

A heart to serve is mandatory for people who want to make a career in helping others. You can't help or lead others if you don't care for them. However, your heart can wear down without some of these other tools in place.

In our time in China, I led a men's group of foreigners who gathered in our city. The purpose was to create a place to be known and to share what was going in our worlds. As we began to develop trust, these men started to share things they didn't want to admit but knew were true.

Each of them came to China out of a deep love for the Chinese people. They had faithfully served them in numerous ways, yet over time some of them mentioned how they have started to hate these same people they were trying to love. These wonderful men knew it was wrong; they didn't want it to be true, but the differences of culture, the slowness to see results, and their own tiredness of spirit led to the unfortunate awareness of hate.

Since these discussions, we have learned that those feelings are not limited to men or simply toward people in other cultures. We began to hear similar attitudes from nurses, teachers, parents, etc. Having the desire to love and serve doesn't necessarily protect us from turning against these same people. We don't want to see this happen to you for the people you feel called to serve.

This Academy of Powerful Caregivers will give you tools to faithfully serve and care for those to whom you feel called. We called this "Powerful Caregivers" because we feel you can give from a place of strength. You have something of value to give. You desire positive change in others, and these tools are designed to give you confidence in your area of service.

Throughout these lessons, I will take a Christian perspective because frankly, that is who I am. I don't take the stance that if you don't believe like I do then you can't effectively serve others. But, as you follow these lessons, you will see ways that God has resourced each of us to effectively help others. It was one of His greatest commandments to love one another. If it is that important to Him, He will help us do it.

Giving Tools Without Addressing the Heart, Delays Healing

When we came to China to help teenage orphan girls, we saw some felt needs they had. When an orphan turned 18 years old, there was no more money given from the State to care for them. In turn, most orphanages would open their doors and let them go.

Even though there is universal education in China, most orphans don't get past 12 years old in school because of no one pushing them to succeed. This severely limits the opportunities for work and to take care of themselves. The boys had opportunities to go into the military; the girls, on the other hand, were limited to possibly working in the orphanage as a housekeeper if a job was available. The majority of orphan girls who age out of the system end up on the street and are vulnerable to being picked up by sex traffickers.

The felt needs of these girls are jobs and education, so we have created a system of skills training to help give these teenage girls a transition from the orphanage to the real world. However, this is really only part of the solution. Giving tools without addressing deeper issues people face only prolongs the problem.

Imagine this example. You have a friend who has a gambling problem, which has led to financial needs for his family. If you give him money to get him back on his feet, would you expect his financial issues to resurface again? Of course, they would because he has not worked on his gambling problem.

People Replicate On The Outside What They Feel On The Inside

For orphans, they feel that nobody wants them; people will always leave them; and they have nothing of value to offer. Giving them tools may increase their belief that they have something to offer, but their basic views of themselves are still negative. These views will cause them to react negatively to others, especially the caregivers.

Let me explain. Orphans often feel that people will eventually leave them. Therefore, if they get to the point of feeling that they care about someone, they may push them away. This seems strange as a caregiver, but from their point of view, it is better to know why the person leaves them than to be kind, loving, and good and still have the person leave. It just doesn't hurt as much.

As a caregiver, we may take these negative reactions as attacks on us or see those we are serving as ungrateful for what we have given. Either view will discourage our willingness to continue serving them. Knowing there are deeper issues involved help us to maintain compassion.

As Christians, we often share the gospel with every project that we create to help others. This creates a dilemma in those we are serving.

1. Are they expected to become a Christian in order to be loved by you?
2. Do they really have value or are they just a project to you?
3. If they never decide to trust Jesus, would you then turn them away? Would you regret having ever helped them?

If we attach conditions to our love and value for people, this creates a very unhealthy start to their view of who Jesus is. Then when they do become a Christian, we may start a lengthy discipleship process teaching them to memorize Scripture, study the Bible, have daily quiet times, etc. We may start pushing them into the Christian mold. There are some people that thrive in this setting, but not everyone does.

There is a longing in each person to be loved for who they are. Unconsciously, we plague those we serve with the idea that only through knowledge and activity will they be loved by us. What happens to their heart when they fail to live up to the standards created? What if they disagree with you? Are we really creating a safe place for them to be all that they were created to be? Or is it only safe if they become what we are creating them to be?

How to Give Lasting Help

The main goal of this chapter is to instruct on how to give lasting help. The way to do this is to give prolonged, persistent, and extravagant love to those you are serving no matter the response you may get.

At first, those you are serving may think you are crazy. Then, they may try to take advantage of you. They may just think you are a nice person. But eventually, by overwhelming them with this love, they will start to believe that maybe they are worthy of love.

The things we say and do are an overflow of what we believe about ourselves and the world around us. We cannot correct the heart through only information. People need to experience the truth before it is truly real for them.

We tend to want to hold people accountable for their mistakes so that they can learn, but God dealt with their mistakes on the cross so He can now overlook them. He doesn't want us to feel that we are collection of the things we do – good or bad. It is His kindness that leads us to repentance, not His punishment (Romans 2:4).

The reason God shines His light on any mistake is not to embarrass us or to punish us, but so that we can bring it to Him to find healing. God is all about getting us better and whole. Punishment and shame were sent to the cross. Healing and new life were sent to us.

Paul's Example of Serving Others

Let's turn now to the Scriptures to see how Paul gave lasting help. Paul here is reminding the Thessalonians about how he served them.

1 Thessalonians 2:1-7a

> [1] You know, brothers and sisters, that our visit to you was not without results. [2] We had previously suffered and been treated outrageously in Philippi, as you know, but with the help of our God we dared to tell you his gospel in the face of strong opposition. [3] For the appeal we make does not spring from error or impure motives, nor are we trying to trick you. [4] On the contrary, we speak as those approved by God to be entrusted with the gospel. We are not trying to please people but God, who tests our hearts. [5] You know we never used flattery, nor did we put on a mask to cover up greed—God is our witness. [6] We were not looking for

praise from people, not from you or anyone else, even though as apostles of Christ we could have asserted our authority. [7] Instead, we were like young children among you.

The first thing I want to point out is that serving people is not always easy. Paul faced strong opposition, and there will be times when you will feel this as well. Serving others takes courage and you will need the help of God (v. 2).

The second thing I want you to notice is that you will be tempted to push people into your point-of-view of things. Paul needed to tell them that he was not trying to trick them because there are others who will (v. 3). You may know what is best for those you are serving, but you cannot force it on them. They have a right to accept you or to reject you. If you take this choice away from them, then you are not serving them; you are controlling them.

The third thing is that the praise of man is a strong lure (v. 4-6). Our focus needs to be on God. Otherwise, the people we are serving will only become a project and not an object of our love.

Finally, Paul said he was like a young child among them (v. 7). In context, this could mean he was without deceit. Our love ought to be sincere. There is no mix of doubt in God's love to us. God's love gives completely without demanding anything in return. If we want our giving to have a lasting effect, we cannot mix any deceit into our love.

Paul goes on in 1 Thessalonians 2:7b-12

> Just as a nursing mother cares for her children, [8] so we
> cared for you. Because we loved you so much, we were
> delighted to share with you not only the gospel of God but
> our lives as well. [9] Surely you remember, brothers and
> sisters, our toil and hardship; we worked night and day in
> order not to be a burden to anyone while we preached the
> gospel of God to you. [10] You are witnesses, and so is God, of
> how holy, righteous and blameless we were among you
> who believed. [11] For you know that we dealt with each of
> you as a father deals with his own children, [12] encouraging,
> comforting and urging you to live lives worthy of God, who
> calls you into his kingdom and glory.

In this section, Paul goes into more detail about how he served
the Thessalonians. He says he was like a mother to them (v. 7).
He loved them enough to share his entire life with the
Thessalonians (v. 8). He didn't put on his ministry hat, share
with them some love, and then move on. He sat with them to
the point where they knew who he was (v. 10). It wasn't just
teaching or information for Paul; it was a total life
transformation. He knew that they needed to see it lived out in
order for them to accept the change for themselves.

Secondly, it wasn't just a job for Paul (v. 9). He worked hard to
not become a burden on those he was serving. Now getting
paid for the service you provide is not wrong, but it does create
an obstacle. Are you serving because you want to, or are you

just trying to make a living? Not having this question mastered will steal from your passion and feed seeds of doubt into those you are serving.

Thirdly, Paul was also like a father to the Thessalonians (v. 11). He was calling them up to something greater than themselves (v. 12). He wasn't trying to make the Thessalonians like himself, but for them to be all that God created them to be. A good father is not trying to replicate himself; he is trying to release his children into their greatest success. It is not about the dad. It's about the child.

Finally, in the last paragraph of chapter 2, Paul continues.

> [17] But, brothers and sisters, when we were orphaned by being separated from you for a short time (in person, not in thought), out of our intense longing we made every effort to see you. [18] For we wanted to come to you—certainly I, Paul, did, again and again—but Satan blocked our way. [19] For what is our hope, our joy, or the crown in which we will glory in the presence of our Lord Jesus when he comes? Is it not you? [20] Indeed, you are our glory and joy.

The first thought here is to reassure the Thessalonians of their place in Paul's affection (v. 20). He may have other great work to do, but they are now a part of him. They are important. They have a place in him.

He goes on to talk about them being his crown in the presence of Jesus (v. 19). There are two main commands Jesus left us: to love God and to love others. As we do these, we honor God with our lives and our rewards will be based on these two. While Paul grew in love with the Thessalonians, his perspective remained in doing it all for the glory of God.

Paul guides us into how to give lasting help as:

1. Your love must be sincere.
2. Your focus is to honor God and not the praise of men.
3. You are not correcting behavior but engaging them to God's heart through your love.
4. You let people see the real you so that they will see Christ in you.
5. You lead people to their destiny, not your vision of their destiny.
6. You stay true to them even when they doubt you.

Additional Resources

Writing things down can be an excellent exercise to help you remember those things you are learning. Use a journal to answer the following questions.

1. What are two things God is highlighting for you about what was in this chapter?

2. How could someone ever turn from loving those they are serving to one day hating them?

3. Think about someone you are serving. What could you change in order to have an even greater impact in their life?

4. For those of you who want to dig deeper into this topic, check out these articles:

   • http://prayer-coach.com/0101/hope
   • http://prayer-coach.com/0101/eulogy

2

How to Trust in the Goodness of God

In the last chapter, we looked at how to give lasting help to others. We talked about how it is not enough to just have a noble desire. If we truly want to give lasting help:

1. Our love must be sincere.
2. Our focus is to honor God and not to gain the praise of men.
3. We are not correcting behavior but engaging them to God's heart through our love.
4. We let people see the real us so that they will see Christ in us.
5. We lead people to their destiny, not our vision of their destiny.
6. We stay true to them even when they doubt us.

This week we will look at how to trust in the goodness of God. As people who want to serve others and give help to them, we will put ourselves in a place to see some of the worst evil of this world. Some of you are helping those in human trafficking. Others of you are working in social services and regularly see children being abused or neglected. Some of you are counselors helping people who have been badly hurt by others. Others of you are in the medical field taking care of those attacked by some disease or sickness.

But we are not just dealing with the evil in this world but the effects of evil on those we are serving. You may be dealing with a woman raising her kids alone because her husband was sent off to war. Maybe the person was in a church where the pastor had a huge public failure and now they don't trust leaders. We see people's pain. We feel their hurt. And, we want to give them something else.

David records his feelings and battles with evil in Psalm 86.

1 Hear me, Lord, and answer me,
   for I am poor and needy.
2 Guard my life, for I am faithful to you;
   save your servant who trusts in you.
   You are my God;
3 have mercy on me, Lord,
   for I call to you all day long.
4 Bring joy to your servant, Lord,
   for I put my trust in you.
5 You, Lord, are forgiving and good,
   abounding in love to all who call to you.
6 Hear my prayer, Lord;
   listen to my cry for mercy.
7 When I am in distress, I call to you,
   because you answer me.

⁸ Among the gods there is none like you, Lord;
no deeds can compare with yours.
⁹ All the nations you have made
will come and worship before you, Lord;
they will bring glory to your name.
¹⁰ For you are great and do marvelous deeds;
you alone are God.
¹¹ Teach me your way, Lord,
that I may rely on your faithfulness;
give me an undivided heart,
that I may fear your name.
¹² I will praise you, Lord my God, with all my heart;
I will glorify your name forever.
¹³ For great is your love toward me;
you have delivered me from the depths,
from the realm of the dead.
¹⁴ Arrogant foes are attacking me, O God;
ruthless people are trying to kill me—
they have no regard for you.
¹⁵ But you, Lord, are a compassionate and gracious God,
slow to anger, abounding in love and faithfulness.
¹⁶ Turn to me and have mercy on me;
show your strength in behalf of your servant;
save me, because I serve you
just as my mother did.
¹⁷ Give me a sign of your goodness,
that my enemies may see it and be put to shame,
for you, Lord, have helped me and comforted me.

Evil can overwhelm us because in reality, without God, we have no hope (Ephesians 2:12). God needs to come through for us to have anything to give to those we are serving. There will be times this will just be a nice thought, but to really love others, there will be times where this "thought" is your lifeline.

There are three things I want to pull from this Psalm. First, David didn't ignore the pain he was feeling. The things he was going through were hurtful and real. Second, David reminds himself of who God is and how great He is. Then, third, David asks for God's help in his situation. In particular, David asks for a sign of His goodness. The path to overcoming evil is by doing good (Romans 12:21).

We Need A Firm Belief In God's Good Intentions For Each Person

Entering into other people's pain can overwhelm you with despair. The only way to maintain hope in the situation is to be grounded in the goodness of God.

> I would have despaired unless I had believed that I would see the goodness of the Lord in the land of the living. - Psalm 27:13

Joseph was hated by his brothers. They were jealous of him for being his father's favorite. Joseph's nighttime dreams of ruling over his brothers added to their insecurities so much so that one day they find him alone away from their father, seize the opportunity, push him into a deep well, and eventually sell him into slavery.

As a slave, Joseph actually did well. He was respected by his owner and was given authority over the business. But, just when things started to rebound for Joseph, he was wrongfully accused of attempted rape and thrown into prison.

Again he did well and gained the respect of the prison manager. He was promoted over all the affairs of the prison. Finally, through a miraculous interpretation of the Pharaoh's dream, he was released from prison and appointed second in command over Egypt.

Some time later, Joseph's brothers came to Egypt – not to celebrate his promotion, but because they were hungry. They came to buy grain because of a severe famine where they lived. They didn't know Joseph was there, but Joseph recognizes them. Through the course of some events, they are reunited.

Joseph's brothers separated him from his father. He was sold into slavery and thrown into prison. He spent years in hardship because of his brothers. After their father's death, they became scared Joseph would punish them for their evil deeds, but Joseph states, "What you intended for evil, God intended for good" (Genesis 50:20). He saw that through it all, God had good intentions for him and for his family.

In the service of others, we will hear terrible things that may have happened to them. They could have been abused by a parent, been a victim of a drug dealer, dropped by a caregiver, ridiculed by classmates, etc. Sympathy will express to them that we identify with their hurt, but it will not give them healing for their pain.

Whatever evil we encounter, we must believe in God's goodness to override it. In the end, evil will not win. We can trust God; He is our hope.

God Manifests His Glory In His Goodness

As the Israelites were roaming the wilderness, Moses is called to go up the mountain to meet with God. In their time together, Moses asked God to show him His glory. God agreed and had all His goodness pass before Moses (Exodus 34:5-6). God's glory, that part of Him that secures praise and renown, is His goodness.

Often we give God credit for His sovereignty by believing that everything is in His control. He could have stopped the evil. We get stuck on questions like, "Why did you let my parents die?" "Why did you let my boyfriend rape me?" "Why did you put me in a family that is poor?" We are so impressed with His sovereignty that we start to blame Him for the evil we experience.

James 1:16-17 tells us that God only gives good gifts. Bad things may happen, but they are not from God. God is in some ways limited by His goodness. And when bad things happen, we have a promise that He will work them for the good for those who love Him (Romans 8:28).

We have a friend whose parents died when she was young. None of her aunts or uncles wanted to take her in so she was raised in an orphanage. She became a Christian and was helping others to know Jesus. One day we were praying with her and asked if she had a question for God. Her answer was, "Why did you not want my family to raise me?"

Her belief in God's sovereignty meant that everything that happened was His will. It is very hard to serve and love a God that would want bad things to happen. We have to believe in His goodness in order for us to have hope.

When people come to us with their problems, we don't have to fix them. We take them to God. We can't say what He will do, but we do know that He is good and He wants to enter into their lives in a real and personal way.

God Created Every Person As A Target For His Love

There is no person that you will meet that God doesn't want His goodness to touch. He created each person to be an object of His love. When He created mankind, He declared us very good (Genesis 1:31). As a caregiver, we need a firm belief in God's good intentions for each person. We need to be able to hear their pain but know God desires good things for them.

I will close with Psalm 73. This Psalm describes the lure of despair over wickedness. It shows our need to remind ourselves of God's goodness. Don't lose heart. God is still good.

[1] Surely God is good to Israel,
to those who are pure in heart.
[2] But as for me, my feet had almost slipped;
I had nearly lost my foothold.
[3] For I envied the arrogant
when I saw the prosperity of the wicked.
[4] They have no struggles;
their bodies are healthy and strong.
[5] They are free from common human burdens;
they are not plagued by human ills.
[6] Therefore pride is their necklace;
they clothe themselves with violence.
[7] From their callous hearts comes iniquity;
their evil imaginations have no limits.
[8] They scoff, and speak with malice;
with arrogance they threaten oppression.
[9] Their mouths lay claim to heaven,
and their tongues take possession of the earth.
[10] Therefore their people turn to them
and drink up waters in abundance.
[11] They say, "How would God know?
Does the Most High know anything?"
[12] This is what the wicked are like—
always free of care, they go on amassing wealth.
[13] Surely in vain I have kept my heart pure
and have washed my hands in innocence.

¹⁴ All day long I have been afflicted,
and every morning brings new punishments.
¹⁵ If I had spoken out like that,
I would have betrayed your children.
¹⁶ When I tried to understand all this,
it troubled me deeply
¹⁷ till I entered the sanctuary of God;
then I understood their final destiny.
¹⁸ Surely you place them on slippery ground;
you cast them down to ruin.
¹⁹ How suddenly are they destroyed,
completely swept away by terrors!
²⁰ They are like a dream when one awakes;
when you arise, Lord,
you will despise them as fantasies.
²¹ When my heart was grieved
and my spirit embittered,
²² I was senseless and ignorant;
I was a brute beast before you.
²³ Yet I am always with you;
you hold me by my right hand.
²⁴ You guide me with your counsel,
and afterward you will take me into glory.
²⁵ Whom have I in heaven but you?
And earth has nothing I desire besides you.
²⁶ My flesh and my heart may fail,
but God is the strength of my heart
and my portion forever.
²⁷ Those who are far from you will perish;
you destroy all who are unfaithful to you.

²⁸ But as for me, it is good to be near God.
   I have made the Sovereign Lord my refuge;
   I will tell of all your deeds.

Many of you feel drawn to help people in a seemly impossible situation. Our calling to teenage orphan girls is huge. There are 14 million orphans that move out of an orphanage each year.[1] They have limited education, limited job skills, few connections, and no family. Out of all the orphans coming out, most websites reference that 10% commit suicide and 40% live on the streets. Out of all the girls, 60% end up in prostitution.[2]

While there are many organizations that help orphans get adopted and many trying to help those caught in sex trafficking, there are few that are working on prevention as these girls transition from the orphanage to live on their own. The numbers alone are overwhelming. The amount of work to make a dent in this situation is overwhelming. We need to depend on the goodness of God to keep us from falling into despair.

When things take longer than we planned... When locals and foreigners tell us that this will not work... When money is running out and we feel forgotten... We need to cling to the goodness of God. He loves these people and has a good plan for them. They were not born to live a life of despair, but one of joy and fulfillment. And with His help, we can make a difference. We depend on His everlasting goodness.

Additional Resources

Writing things down can be an excellent exercise to help you remember those things you are learning. Use a journal to answer the following questions.

1. What are two things God is highlighting for you about what was in this chapter?

2. What do you think you are more likely to see in other people's lives, the goodness of God for them or the evils of this world?

    *   If you thought evils, what would it take for the goodness of God to become more likely?

3. Think about someone you are serving. What is a way to bring hope into their life in relation to the goodness of God?

4. For those of you who want to dig deeper into this topic, check out this article:

- http://prayer-coach.com/0102/good-mood

3

How to Trust in the Goodness of Man

We need to cling to the goodness of God, so we don't fall into despair over the evil and difficulties we experience. However, to effectively serve others we also need to trust in the goodness of man in the midst of the pain, hurt, and evil we will see. In the last chapter, we looked at how to trust in the goodness of God; this chapter will show how we can trust in the goodness of man.

When Service is No Longer Fun

Each of you feels the pull to help others otherwise you would not be interested in this course. Still, how you got to this point may be different for each of you. Maybe you had a parent who modeled this for you. Maybe you have experienced the joy of helping others and find it rewarding. Maybe you had a rough life and want to keep others from that same pain you felt. Maybe you truly don't know.

I feel that it is important to be secure in why you want to help others. Again, as in the goodness of God, when the pressures of life come in and helping others becomes no longer fun, being confident in why you are doing what you are doing keeps you in the game.

Nearing the end of his ministry, Jesus started to head toward Jerusalem. But on the way, He needed to pass through Samaria. Jesus sent messengers ahead to prepare things for Him, but the people there did not welcome Him.

The disciples had been following Jesus for about three years. They had ministered alongside him healing people, feeding people, and watching all that Jesus did. Now, after being rejected by the people in this Samarian town, Peter and John wanted to call down fire to destroy it (Luke 9:54).

Several years ago, my wife and I took on a few college students. We poured our love into them during a retreat that we felt would be helpful to them. We treated them as if they were our own family, and they loved us back. It was a great trip – one that we still look back on fondly for each of these students.

When we returned, one student decided to make accusations against us to our leadership. It made life hard for about a month before it all came to nothing. However the following year this student tanked, broke most of her Christian relationships and moved in with her boyfriend.

The temptation is to feel vindicated... she got what she deserved.

I bring this up because not everyone will receive your service. Does other people's rejection of you release you from the obligation to love them? You will have to make a choice based on what you believe to be true. Are you only going to love those that deserve to be loved, or will you be able to keep on loving through the pain? Or to ask the question differently, do you want to make a lasting impact on others or do you want to make a temporary impact that can only last as long as other people appreciate what you give?

God Put His Goodness In Each Of Us

Just as we need to cling to the goodness of God, I also believe we need to cling to the goodness in man.

When God originally made us, God said that we were very good (Genesis 1:31). Each person has woven into their very DNA the goodness of God. Nobody was created to be bad, to be a failure, or to ruin the lives of those around them.

It is true that there is sin in the world. But, sin came after God created man. God put goodness inside man, and then sin distorted the original plan. So while everyone does have a sin problem, there is still good in them.

Jesus didn't come to remove the evil and put in the good; He came to remove the evil so that the good could fully shine (Isaiah 60:1).

When we are called to love others, this is the part we are called to connect with. We are to connect with the goodness that God placed there. We are not loving the parts that could be there if only they would come to Jesus; we are loving that good part of them that already God put there and wants to shine forth.

When God created us, He placed a part of His glory in us. That part shines forth the goodness of God in a way that no one else can. As you honor and love this part of people, even when they are not believers, you get to experience a part of God's glory that you could have otherwise missed.

We Were Meant For Glory

Let me elaborate more on this point. One of the primary verses we memorize as a new believer is Romans 3:23. It tells us that we have all sinned and fall short of the glory of God. The reason we get people to memorize this verse is to make sure they know all have sinner so then they we realize that they need a savior.

The second half of that verse is used to further explain how we have all sinned. The way I was taught to explain it is to think of the glory of God as perfection. Therefore anytime we didn't reach perfection, then that would be sin. Have you been perfect in everything?

Then we launch into that person's need of a savior and how Jesus paid the penalty of sin. I am not arguing with the logic or the importance to that way of thinking. However, God's glory is not some abstract view of perfection. We were intended to live life in such a way to bring God glory in all that we do.

Jesus was able to do this. He was without sin (Hebrews 4:15), so He was able to attain to the glorifying God through His life. He was the radiance of God's glory and the exact representation of His being (Hebrew 1:3).

While we cannot attain to the glory of God without Jesus, there is something inside each of us that looks to radiate God's glory for ourselves. Sometimes we focus so much on the sinfulness of man that we forget there is something in each of us wanting to reflect the goodness of God. Remember, we are all made in the image of God.

Can Non-Christians Be Good?

I used to have a hard time with thinking there was good in non-Christians. As a teenager, I even thought that my dad was not a good father because he was not a Christian. I believed in the depravity of man to the degree that no one without Jesus was good.

In reality, I had a very good father. He was always at any sporting thing I was doing. He even helped coach some of those teams. He would play with me outside, even coming up with games that he would play with my brother and me. I grew out of this poor view of my dad, yet as a teenager, this belief put a great amount of tension between us.

There is much good in the world done by people who don't know God. Are those good things tainted with sin? Yes. But, I also know much of the good I do now as a believer is still tainted.

Here is a short list of men that brought good in our world, which I can find no evidence that they were Christians:

- Thomas Jefferson
- Alexander Graham Bell
- Thomas Edison
- Henry Ford
- Wright Brothers
- Gandhi
- Walt Disney
- Tim Berners-Lee
- Steve Jobs
- George Lucas

God wants all of us to reach our full potential because we each have something good to bring to our world. He wants us to stop falling short of His glory, because when He created us, He placed a part of His glory in us to be represented through us.

As you honor and love this part of people, even when they are not believers, you get to experience a part of God's glory that you could have otherwise missed. People start to believe in themselves once they experience other people believing in them. Ideally, this would have come from their parents, but that doesn't happen for everyone. You have the privilege to call someone else to the greatness God put in them.

How Jesus Treated People in the Gospels

This is how Jesus treated people in the Gospels. He didn't draw attention to sin unless it was hindering others from coming to God, Pharisees. Normally He allowed His kindness to draw people to repentance (Romans 2:4). He calls us all to become all we were created to be.

This is how Jesus treated Zacchaeus (Luke 19:1-10). Zacchaeus was the tax collector of his town. He cheated his neighbors to become quite wealthy. He worked for the evil foreigners who were ruling over them. Because of this, most people didn't like him.

Jesus comes to town. He spots Zacchaeus in a tree and asks to be welcomed in his home. The townspeople are frustrated. Jesus, the religious celebrity, chose to dine with the famous sinner from their town.

Throughout their interaction, Jesus never mentions Zacchaeus' sin. He doesn't condemn Zacchaeus. He doesn't even make subtle comments about his wealth. Jesus just honors Zacchaeus with His presence and fellowship.

Next thing we see is Zacchaeus offering to give half of his possessions to the poor and give back four times what he has cheated from others.

In the presence of true love and acceptance, the goodness in Zacchaeus rises up to where he desires to do the right thing.

God Commands Us To Love Each Other to Release More Of His Glory

It might not work this quick on people we serve, but we must believe that the goodness is there. If we have a hard time finding that goodness in someone, let's ask God what it is. He wants to show us because that goodness was placed there for His glory.

We bring God glory as we reveal that goodness that God has put in each of us. As we see this in others, focus on it, and call it out of others, we are releasing more of God's glory in the world and sin has less of a foothold.

I have found that people generally have a hard time seeing the good in themselves. While they may agree with this concept for others, they doubt it for themselves. We believe that if people really got to know us then they would be scared off. We know the thoughts in our heads and the things that we do, and we can't imagine anything really good in that.

What we don't realize is that our call to love our neighbor as ourselves requires us to actually love ourselves. As we start believing the good in ourselves, we become more fully convinced of the good in others – no matter how deeply it is buried. But let's look at that commandment again.

The Second is Like the First

> Jesus replied: "'Love the Lord your God with all your heart
> and with all your soul and with all your mind.' This is the
> first and greatest commandment. And the second is like it:
> 'Love your neighbor as yourself.' All the Law and the
> Prophets hang on these two commandments." - Matthew
> 22:37-40

Jesus made it clear that there were two things that were
important if we wanted to follow Him: love God and love
others. What is strange is how the second is like the first. How
is 'loving your neighbor' like 'loving God'?

We often miss this connection because we have a limited view
of what 'loving our neighbor' should look like. We often limit
this to just doing good things for others. If we see someone in
need, we should help them. While this is part of it, if we limit
our view to just helps, we miss the bigger command to love.

Part of loving others is getting to know them. As we listen to
others, we can start to see the greatness God put in them. God
is so extremely creative and loving that He has placed a little
bit of Himself in each person. As we love that person we get to
experience that piece of God for ourselves.

The point is that when we go deeper with people, we are
exposing ourselves to more of God. As we get to know others
we test what we actually believe about God.

- Do we feel that we can comfort others, or do we remain silent when others are hurting (2 Corinthians 1:4)?
- Do we believe we are accepted in our weaknesses, or do we hide our faults for fear of being rejected (2 Corinthians 12:9)?
- Do we believe in God's protection, or do we refuse to forgive others when they hurt us (Colossians 3:13)?

The truth is that we cannot fully love God without loving others. And, we cannot fully love others without getting to know them enough in order to know how to love them. And, if we get close enough to know them, then there is a good chance that we may get hurt by them, and so we will need to pull even more on our love for God to continue to love them.

If we believe in the goodness of man, will we get hurt? Sometimes. Will people take advantage of us? Most likely. Will people think you are foolish? Absolutely.

But here is the thing. "Who is going to harm you if you are eager to do good? But even if you should suffer for what is right, you are blessed" (1 Peter 3:13-14). People may not receive your goodness towards them. They may not believe in the goodness that God put in them. But, you are not really doing it for them; you are serving the Lord.

Let me remind you of Colossians 3:23-24:

> "Whatever you do, work at it with all your heart, as working for the Lord, not for human masters, since you know that you will receive an inheritance from the Lord as a reward. It is the Lord Christ you are serving."

If you do what is good, you will be blessed. You will receive an inheritance. You will receive a reward. What can man do to you that God cannot outgive back to you as a reward?

There is good in each person because God put it there. Call it out of them. Believe that it will come out. Do it long enough and honestly enough until they start to believe that they really have goodness in them.

Additional Resources

Writing things down can be an excellent exercise to help you remember those things you are learning. Use a journal to answer the following questions.

1. What are two things God is highlighting for you about what was in this chapter?

2. What are some of the things God put in you to express His goodness?

3. Think about someone you are serving. What is something amazing about them that they would be encouraged if you told them?

4. For those of you who want to dig deeper into this topic, check out this article:

   • http://prayer-coach.com/0103/like

4

How to Have Empathy Without Losing Hope

The people we serve will not always be nice to us. In fact, they may reject us.

The stories that they share of the evil done to them may also discourage our hope in man. We need to hold fast to our belief that there is goodness in every person, so we won't allow our awareness of evil to taint our love and service.

Clinging to the goodness of God and man is important, but there is still a tendency to lose hope. The problems we will face at times are overwhelming. You may work with a family whose child has cancer. You may work with a girl who was gang raped by her high school classmates. You may work with a guy who finds out his wife is pregnant with someone else's kid.

There is a lot of pain in the world. There are plenty of examples of injustice and plain evil. As caregivers, we walk into a world of hurt and are expected to bring hope.

We Need God's Perspective In Our Service To Others

The book of Job tells of how Job in a very quick order loses his wealth, kids, and health. He then has his wife turn on him as well. Three of Job's friends decide to comfort him. When they get there, for the first seven days all they could do was sit with him and cry (Job 2:11-13).

That was a great start, but these friends then decided to give Job their thoughts of the situation. They tell Job that it must have been his fault for his pain and struggles. In an attempt to protect God's reputation, they attacked Job. They reasoned that it couldn't be God's fault, so it must be Job's.

We have to be careful with our help, that we don't actually make things worse. Things are not always what we can see. Only God's perspective can properly lead us in effective service to others.

There is a story of two women who both had newborn babies. During the night one of the women rolls over on her child and accidentally kills it. As the other woman slept, she realizes what happened and switches the babies. In the morning the other woman awakes, notices the dead baby next to her, and realizes this dead baby is not actually her child.

Some of you already know this story and where it is heading, but try to imagine what both women are going through. While the one mother whose child had died was being selfish in switching the babies, she still suffered an unexpected and unfair tragedy.

Obviously, the mother whose baby was still alive had a greater injustice done to her. Both were scared. Some people in their mercy would have suggested that they both raise the child. Others in their justice would suggest the mother of the dead child should be put in prison.

In this case, the person helping the two women was King Solomon, and he was the judge between them. He orders the child to be cut in two so that each woman could have half. The woman, whose child it was, was horrified and said the other woman could have him. The mother of the dead child believed the verdict was good, and neither of them would have a child.

Solomon immediately knew the mother of the living child (1 Kings 3:16-28).

Solomon is credited with being a wise ruler. This may seem unfair to set this as an example for you, but when we cling to the goodness of God, we need to account for the potential of the supernatural help. This is the major difference between Solomon and Job's friends. Solomon allowed God to give supernatural guidance; Job's friends relied only on what they could comprehend or was logical to them.

Our Focus Is On God And His Love For Each Person

As we move toward people, we need to stay in a place of awareness of God's goodness so that their pain doesn't overwhelm us. If we focus on their problem, our best service to them would be to help them cope with that problem. If we focus on God and listen to Him, we will have something full of life to offer them.

After Jesus had resurrected, Peter and John were walking through Jerusalem and came upon a man who had been crippled since birth begging for money. Peter looked at the man and said that they didn't have money but would give him what they had. Peter then declared, "in the name of Jesus Christ of Nazareth, walk" (Acts 3:1-8).

You may not feel comfortable telling a crippled person to walk, but the point is they gave what they had. That applies to us as well. We need to know what God has put in us to freely give away to others.

2 Corinthians 4:1 helps to give us clarity on this.

> Therefore, since through God's mercy we have this ministry, we do not lose heart.

Stop. Paul immediately declares we do not lose heart. Let this sink in because it implies that if you allow yourself to go unchecked, you would lose heart. Paul continues about sharing the gospel, but let's jump down to verse 7.

[7] But we have this treasure in jars of clay to show that this all-surpassing power is from God and not from us. [8] We are hard pressed on every side, but not crushed; perplexed, but not in despair; [9] persecuted, but not abandoned; struck down, but not destroyed.[10] We always carry around in our body the death of Jesus, so that the life of Jesus may also be revealed in our body. [11] For we who are alive are always being given over to death for Jesus' sake, so that his life may also be revealed in our mortal body. [12] So then, death is at work in us, but life is at work in you.

The pressures of this world cause us to be hard-pressed, perplexed, persecuted, and struck down, but we are not crushed, not in despair, not abandoned, and not destroyed because we carry around in us the resurrected life of Jesus. We experience these pains because we are always being given over to death for Jesus' sake.

We all want to make an impact in others' lives. But it is not through an easy life that people see Jesus living through us. The life of Jesus is revealed in our body by our connection with tiny deaths – emotional, physical, and spiritual deaths.

We choose to be handed over to death so that those we are serving have life rise up in them. The death of Jesus was the ultimate display of love, and as His followers, we die to ourselves that those we serve may live.

We Don't Let Pain Consume Us

Let's continue on at verse 13.

> [13] It is written: "I believed; therefore I have spoken." Since we have that same spirit of faith, we also believe and therefore speak, [14] because we know that the one who raised the Lord Jesus from the dead will also raise us with Jesus and present us with you to himself. [15] All this is for your benefit, so that the grace that is reaching more and more people may cause thanksgiving to overflow to the glory of God.

> [16] Therefore we do not lose heart. [AGAIN] Though outwardly we are wasting away, yet inwardly we are being renewed day by day. [17] For our light and momentary troubles are achieving for us an eternal glory that far outweighs them all. [18] So we fix our eyes not on what is seen, but on what is unseen, since what is seen is temporary, but what is unseen is eternal.

We are not dying for dying sake. No! We know that outwardly we are wasting away, but inwardly we are being renewed day by day. Daily, we are being filled up with more of Jesus.

How are we renewed? By not looking at what is seen. If we keep our eyes on the problems, we will waste away. But as we look to what is unseen, to what is eternal, to what God is doing, we will be renewed every day. We will not lose hope because He is our hope.

Now starting in chapter 5...

> ¹ For we know that if the earthly tent we live in is destroyed, we have a building from God, an eternal house in heaven, not built by human hands. ² Meanwhile we groan, longing to be clothed instead with our heavenly dwelling, ³ because when we are clothed, we will not be found naked. ⁴ For while we are in this tent, we groan and are burdened, because we do not wish to be unclothed but to be clothed instead with our heavenly dwelling, so that what is mortal may be swallowed up by life. ⁵ Now the one who has fashioned us for this very purpose is God, who has given us the Spirit as a deposit, guaranteeing what is to come.

All of the deaths we experience are moving us to have more and more of our mortal body and thinking to be swallowed up by abundant life. Those deaths transform us because, through them, we experience more of the life of Jesus in us. This is why God gave us the Holy Spirit, so we can start to experience the life that is to come.

Let's continue down in verse 14...

> ¹⁴ For Christ's love compels us, because we are convinced that one died for all, and therefore all died. ¹⁵ And he died for all, that those who live should no longer live for themselves but for him who died for them and was raised again.

[16] So from now on we regard no one from a worldly point of view. Though we once regarded Christ in this way, we do so no longer. [17] Therefore, if anyone is in Christ, the new creation has come: The old has gone, the new is here! [18] All this is from God, who reconciled us to himself through Christ and gave us the ministry of reconciliation: [19] that God was reconciling the world to himself in Christ, not counting people's sins against them. And he has committed to us the message of reconciliation. [20] We are therefore Christ's ambassadors, as though God were making his appeal through us. We implore you on Christ's behalf: Be reconciled to God. [21] God made him who had no sin to be sin for us, so that in him we might become the righteousness of God.

Why do we put ourselves through all of this? Why are we dying to ourselves to minister to others? The love of Christ compels us. We have been given the ministry of reconciliation. We know what it was like to live apart from God, and now that we have been brought in, we implore others to be reconciled.

No one has to live separated from God. All of the problems of this world fade away in light of the surpassing knowledge of Christ in us. All the trouble and hardship is transformed in Christ. We can look at other people's troubles and know God can take care of that. We may not know how, but we have experienced enough of His transformation within us that we are convinced He will also do it for them.

This compels us on in love. God has a solution for every problem.

If our futures were not secured and satisfied by God, then we would be excessively anxious. We would live in paralyzing fear or in self-managed, greedy control. We would end up thinking about ourselves, our future, our problems and our potential, and that would keep us from loving others.

But, our hope in Christ is the birthplace of our self-sacrificing love. That's because we are no longer preoccupied with ourselves and can trust in God to take care of us. Since we know God will be there for us, we can venture towards others to be there for them.

Serving others is not about us, so that releases the pressure off of us to perform. We can just love others and give room for God to show up in their lives. We don't need the right answers or need to see some change in the other person. Our goal is to love them as if God were loving them through us.

As we remember it is not all about us, we are free to continue to serve no matter the response we receive. Our work is not to please man or to satisfy some inner longing within us; our work is an act of sacrifice to God (Colossians 3:23). We are not tempted to give up serving others because we know it is the right thing to do, we know it will produce life, and we know we will be rewarded by God for our service. Therefore we don't lose heart.

Additional Resources

Writing things down can be an excellent exercise to help you remember those things you are learning. Use a journal to answer the following questions.

1. What are two things God is highlighting for you about what was in this chapter?

2. What is something you can hold onto so you will not lose hope?

3. Think about someone you are serving. Imagine what it would look like if life were to rise up in them?

4. For those of you who want to dig deeper into this topic, check out this article:

    •   http://prayer-coach.com/0104/afraid

5

How to Love Others

As Christians, love is an overarching theme, which leads us to want to help others. But, there will be times when the pressures of this world override our awareness of God's goodness and our belief in the goodness in others. Sometimes we just have to love because it is the thing to do.

Romans 12:9 tells us love must be sincere. And, we want this too. We want love to flow naturally from our being, but we have to train our bodies to do this. We want to love because we truly love. Sure, loving when we don't feel like it is better than hating others, but sincere love paves the way for the Holy Spirit to freely flow into others.

God Always Helps Us Do What He Ask Us To Do

The first thing we need to remember is to not feel like we are left alone in this process.

New York Times bestselling author, Ted Dekker, shares his journey in giving out of God's love in his book, Waking Up[1]. He shares of his desire to receive love and acceptance. He knew God valued those who loved well.

In his words:

> Jesus' teaching was clear: any sinner can show love to those who love them, but true love shows kindness to those who are cruel and dishonoring to you. Paul was plain: true love holds no record of wrong... Love was the greatest power of any, I saw.
>
> So I pressed in hard, determined to be the one who would succeed in earning God's favor by loving as He asked me to love.
>
> But no matter how hard I tried to submit myself to God, I wasn't able to love in this way. No really. I tried, but in my heart, where it really matters, I was offended by those who were mean and lashed out against me and I judged them in return, thus failing to show true love without which all else was worthless.
>
> I never doubted my standing in the next life, but I often felt shame in this life, constantly disappointing God in my failure to love as He asked me to love.

How many of us are like this? We want to love as God has asked us to, but we realize that the task is too hard. How do we consistently love others?

Dekker fought with this question for 15 years. He would write books on God's love and power but feel powerless and unloving trying to apply them in his own life. He knew what the Bible promised, but he struggled to live it out. That is until God showed up. This is what Dekker writes:

> I remember that day so clearly. There in my office, drowning in a sea of self-condemnation and unworthiness, a gentle question whispered through my mind.
>
> 'Does your Father in Heaven not love you with the same love that He asks you to love others?'
>
> I blinked, unable to comprehend. The room went utterly still.
>
> What is love?
>
> But I knew, of course. Love was a staggering concept that held no record of wrong and was kind to those who hate. Love was the fruit of the Spirit by which all God's children would be known. Love was what I had failed at...
>
> Has your Father failed to love you in this way?
>
> I sat in my chair, stunned, unable to accept the implication that anyone could possibly love me in such a way. I had never thought to ask God to love me the way He asks me to love others.

This really is the first and main thing to consider when approaching the question about how to love others... that God is not asking anything of you that He does want to give to you.

- We love because He loved us (1 John 4:19).
- We forgive because He forgave us (Colossians 3:13).
- We comfort others because He has comforted us (2 Corinthians 1:3).
- We give to God because He gave to us first (Deuteronomy 16:17).

Paul states it this way in Philippians 2:12-13:

[12] Therefore, my dear friends, ... continue to work out your salvation with fear and trembling, [13] for it is God who works in you to will and to act in order to fulfill his good purpose.

We Love Others Because God Loves Us

Knowing that we love out of the love given to us, there are two things that help us live out of the love He has given.

The first is found in Luke 7:36-50.

[36] When one of the Pharisees invited Jesus to have dinner with him, he went to the Pharisee's house and reclined at the table. [37] A woman in that town who lived a sinful life learned that Jesus was eating at the Pharisee's house, so she came there with an alabaster jar of perfume. [38] As she stood behind him at his feet weeping, she began to wet his

feet with her tears. Then she wiped them with her hair, kissed them and poured perfume on them.

[39] When the Pharisee who had invited him saw this, he said to himself, "If this man were a prophet, he would know who is touching him and what kind of woman she is—that she is a sinner."

[40] Jesus answered him, "Simon, I have something to tell you."

"Tell me, teacher," he said.

[41] "Two people owed money to a certain moneylender. One owed him five hundred denarii, and the other fifty. [42] Neither of them had the money to pay him back, so he forgave the debts of both. Now which of them will love him more?"

[43] Simon replied, "I suppose the one who had the bigger debt forgiven."

"You have judged correctly," Jesus said.

[44] Then he turned toward the woman and said to Simon, "Do you see this woman? I came into your house. You did not give me any water for my feet, but she wet my feet with her tears and wiped them with her hair. [45] You did not give me a kiss, but this woman, from the time I entered, has not stopped kissing my feet. [46] You did not put oil on my head, but she has poured perfume on my

feet. ^{47} Therefore, I tell you, her many sins have been forgiven—as her great love has shown. But whoever has been forgiven little loves little."

^{48} Then Jesus said to her, "Your sins are forgiven."

^{49} The other guests began to say among themselves, "Who is this who even forgives sins?"

^{50} Jesus said to the woman, "Your faith has saved you; go in peace."

Let's start with the obvious. Our love for God is motivated by His kindness towards us. Our gratefulness for how He overcame our sin and weaknesses to bestow His love on us compels us to love Him too.

But let's look a little deeper at this. Both Simon and the woman wanted to be with Jesus, and Jesus was wanting to be with them. Simon invited Jesus to his home, and Jesus came. The woman wanted to be at Jesus' feet, and He let her. Most of us don't have more of Jesus because we don't ask for more.

We think that the woman loved Jesus more because she was forgiven of more. That is a dangerous trap. That line of thinking will make you want to go live a reckless lifestyle just so you can love God more for His forgiveness.

We know that the Pharisees had more harsh words spoken to them than the normal sinners. Simon more than likely was just as much a sinner as the woman, yet he didn't know it. The point is when we realize the extent to which Jesus came to us (how much of a sinner we really were), we will be overwhelmed with love for Him.

We need this awareness in order to love others because if we are so unsettled with our need of Jesus, we cannot love others well. We are to love our neighbor as we love ourselves (Luke 10:27). The command is not to love others *more than* ourselves but to love them *as* we love ourselves. If we think we are basically good without need of God or think that we are basically too bad for God, we will not have a healthy love for ourselves, and so we will not love others well.

The second thing we need in order to live out of this love God has given us is found in 1 John 5:14-15.

> [14] This is the confidence we have in approaching God: that if we ask anything according to his will, he hears us. [15] And if we know that he hears us—whatever we ask—we know that we have what we asked of him.

If we fully understand this verse, we will be released into new levels of freedom in Christ in many areas of our lives. John is telling us that we can have the confidence to get what we ask for in prayer if we ask for things that are according to His will. This gives us boldness in our prayers.

Now this caveat, 'according to His will,' may dispel some of your boldness, but God tells us those things that are according to His will. And in relation to this lesson, since God has commanded us to love one another (Romans 13:8), if we pray for the ability to love someone else, then we can have the confidence that we have received that for which we have asked.

If we ask to be able to love, we can move forward in faith knowing that love will flow to us from God to be able to love that person. It doesn't matter how hard it is to love that person, the love will come and we can have confidence in that.

Actually, I find this is a way God likes to work. He likes for us to do something beyond our provisions, power, and resources so that He will have to show up for us. It is the displays of faith that get God's attention (Luke 7:9).

- There is no ram until you are about to bring down the knife (Genesis 22:10-13).
- The river becomes dry once you put your foot in (Joshua 3:15).
- The wall doesn't fall until you shout (Joshua 6:20).
- Your skin doesn't become clean until you wash the seventh time (2 Kings 5:14).
- The fish and loaves multiply as they are handing them out (Luke 9:10-17).
- You can walk on the water after you get out of the boat (Matthew 14:29).
- The crippled man doesn't walk until you tell him to stand up (Acts 3:6-7).

God really enjoys our faith. He looks for people who have faith (Luke 18:8). It is impossible to please Him without faith. He rewards faith (Hebrews 11:6).

We can serve people well. We can help meet all of their needs. We can heal their wounds. We can do all of this, but if we don't have love, we will not be effective in serving them (1 Corinthians 13:1-3). Loving others can be hard. On our own it can feel impossible. Allow these three reminders help you in your quest to love:

1. God helps us to love. He wants to give us what He commands of us.
2. Awareness of His forgiveness to us helps us to love others.
3. Love is always available by faith.

Additional Resources

Writing things down can be an excellent exercise to help you remember those things you are learning. Use a journal to answer the following questions.

1. What are two things God is highlighting for you about what was in this chapter?

2. What is something you can do to increase your love for God?

3. Think about someone you are serving that is hard for you to love. What are some things that God loves about them?

4. For those of you who want to dig deeper into this topic, check out this article:

    •   http://prayer-coach.com/0105/increase

6

How to Greatly Increase Your Love For Others

In the last chapter, we looked at how it is difficult to love others, but we can find strength in these three things:

1. God helps us to love. He wants to give us what He commands of us.
2. Awareness of His forgiveness to us helps us to love others.
3. Love is always available by faith.

It is so easy to get misdirected in how we feel about others. Something happens to tick us off. They rub us the wrong way. We get defensive. And, we then withhold our love.

When we get convicted of our attitude, we can remind ourselves of how much God has forgiven our offenses so we can die to self and choose to love by faith trusting that God will give us love for this person. But there is one step that I have found that adds to this process.

How Did Ananias Have Courage to Speak to Saul?

The one thing I would add to how to greatly increase your love for others is to hear what God is saying about them.

Think about Saul before his conversion. If there was one person the Christians could have pointed at as someone from whom to withhold their love, this would be the man. We know that he stood with those that stoned Stephen. By looking after the clothes of those stoning, he was saying he condoned their actions and took full responsibility for the stoning (Acts 7:58).

Saul then took to disbanding all Christians. He went from home to home dragging out both men and women putting them in prison (Acts 8:3). He willingly tore apart families under the conviction that followers of Jesus needed to be punished for their ways. After scattering the Christians in Jerusalem, he got permission to do the same in Damascus (Acts 9:1-2).

We know the story. On the way to Damascus, Jesus meets with him and confronts him on his persecution. Saul is left blinded by the experience.

The Lord then meets with Ananias, a Christian in Damascus. Jesus tells him to go to Saul to restore his sight. Ananias didn't want to go.

The man who had done great harm to the Christians was struck down. Wasn't this cause for great rejoicing? Maybe this was what most Christians were praying for?

But as Christians we can't rejoice at our enemies' destruction. We are called to love them, which means we greatly desire good for them (Matthew 3:43-45).

Still Ananias needed God's view of Saul before he went, for he not only knew Saul's reputation, he knew that Saul was coming to arrest Christians. That meant Ananias was in danger.

> But the Lord said to Ananias, "Go! This man is my chosen instrument to proclaim my name to the Gentiles and their kings and to the people of Israel" (Acts 9:15).

Basically God said, "Yes, I know what he has been doing, but he is still important to me. I have a purpose for him. Trust me and help him be who I called him to be."

How Did Peter Change His Mind About Gentiles?

Peter had a similar experience in the very next chapter. He had a prejudice against the Gentiles and in particular to Roman soldiers. Nothing personal against Peter, all Jews pretty much felt this way. The Law was given to the Jews; they were God's special people, set apart for Him. And, the Romans were the occupying force over them. Many had hoped the Messiah was going to come to overthrow the Romans. Then add on top of this normal dislike, Peter saw the Romans beat Jesus, ridicule Him, and eventually hang Him on a cross.

Peter had heard Jesus' words about loving your enemies and being kind to those who mistreat you, but he didn't know he was still being unloving. He thought nothing was wrong with never entering a Gentile's home, and he never thought the Gospel was also good news for them.

God blindsided Peter with a vision where God wanted him to eat unclean animals. It's funny that when God's voice is unexpected, we often assume we misheard Him. Peter's response was, "No, Lord." God shows Peter this same vision three times followed each time with Peter's denial. God finally has to be blunt telling him there are some men downstairs, and He didn't want Peter to hesitate going with them.

Peter's view of Gentiles was so ingrained that he would have missed what God was doing without God's intervention. Peter does go with the men and enters the home of the Roman centurion. Peter says, "I now realize how true it is that God does not show favoritism but accepts from every nation the one who fears him and does what is right" (Acts 10:34-35).

We may know the Scriptures and follow all the Christian rules, and yet still miss what God is saying to us. The Old Testament told us not to associate with sinners, but Jesus came and spent most of His time with the prostitutes and tax collectors. I'm not suggesting we should go hang out in strip clubs and drug parties, but we do need to leave room for God to send us where He wants us to go.

We set up rules to make life easier. Within the confines of rules, we know what is expected of us and we can't be held accountable for our decisions... because we are following the rules. But we are not called to follow rules; we are called to follow God. We are not to live by bread alone, but by every word that proceeds from the mouth of God (Matthew 4:4).

This is how we are to love others. We should not create a distinction between people that we will like and people we will distrust. We need to hear the voice of God in order to relate to people the way God wants us to relate to them.

What Did Samuel See In Saul To Make Him King?

Often the people we are called to love will not see themselves as worthy of the love you are offering. In the Old Testament, there is another Saul. He lost some of his father's donkeys and decides to go to the man of God for help finding them.

As Saul was entering the town, the man of God, Samuel, saw him and God told him that Saul would be the one he was to anoint as ruler of Israel. Samuel invites Saul to dine with him and tells him, not to worry about the donkeys; they have already been found. And adds that Saul was the man all of Israel has placed their hope (1 Samuel 9:20).

Saul is perplexed. He tells Samuel that he is a nobody. He is from the smallest clan of the smallest tribe of Israel. He doesn't deserve such grand words.

Saul, however, decides to stay with Samuel. Samuel honors him with food, time, and attention. Before departing, Samuel anoints Saul as king over Israel. With all the love and attention from Samuel, as they leave each other, Saul's heart is changed (1 Samuel 10:9).

That's what love does. It believes in people until they can believe in themselves. Saul had many ups and down in believing what God said about him. These doubts led to mistakes and eventually cost him the place as king over Israel.

This is actually a good example for us. We don't know how people will respond to our love, but that shouldn't change us from being open to them. Our heart should always desire for their well-being. Ananias could have rejoiced at (New Testament) Saul's blindness and refused to give him the gift of restored sight. Instead he trusted God and now we have a collection of Scripture written by this same man that leads us in our understanding of God.

How to Greatly Increase Your Love For Others

I've led men's groups for many years, and I've had many types of guys come through. Some enjoy the interaction, give to others their time and attention, and make the group pleasurable. Others are needy and want to be the center of attention. Others come but try to hide in the background. And some make you question if you want to continue leading groups because they make the whole time frustrating.

I had one guy like this. He used time in the group to say how he didn't like the way I was leading. He told others what he thought they needed to do. And, he would actively go against whatever we were doing as a group.

The immediate reaction to someone like this is to quickly remove him from the group. It is not worth having one person ruin the benefits for everyone else. But before I took this measure, I had my wife pray about him. (Honestly, my wife needed to pray because I wanted him gone.)

What she felt about this man was that he was like a little plant in God's hands and God was looking for a place to plant it so it could grow. This didn't change the man's behaviors, but it did change my attitude toward him. I felt that God was giving me an opportunity, and because of this, I was more willing to look for this man's goodness though his gifts, strengths, and character. I did have to talk to him about how he was affecting the group, which gratefully he was willing to work on.

It wasn't easy having him in the group even after this, but the point is that on our own we will too quickly give up on people. We need to hear about people from God's viewpoint.

There was another guy I had in a group that was nice in the group setting, but he also didn't believe in the direction of the group, in particular the need for men to be vulnerable with each other. The community aspect kept him coming, but I could tell that he wasn't on board. As I prayed about how God saw this man, I felt God said he was a very kind man and loved people well. I kept telling him this and affirming him in this way.

Slowly he started responding to my acceptance and encouragement of him. After several weeks, he decided to share something that happened to him over 50 years prior. He never shared it with anyone else and was highly embarrassed by it. The group prayed for him and affirmed him. He felt relief and said it was the best night of his life. After this, he became the biggest promoter of the group and an important catalyst for sharing between the men.

It is too easy to miss the blessings of other people by focusing on their outward appearances. Remember God's word to Samuel, "People look at the outward appearance, but the Lord looks at the heart" (1 Samuel 16:7). And God loves to tell you what He thinks of other people because He wants to help you love them the way that He does.

If you ask God to show you something about someone and it doesn't draw you to love them more, then you haven't listened to God long enough. There are people that are not safe, but every person has qualities that are lovely – we may just have to look harder for those qualities.

There is a difference between how people act and believe about themselves, and how God created them to be. We are called to dive into those hidden areas that are more real than the behaviors we see in others. If you don't get anything specific information from God about the person, you can always revert to the general words God says about everyone (e.g. they are worthy of love, God has a plan for them, God will never leave them). Either way you have enough ammunition to fully love people all the time.

The enemy is constantly telling people that they are less than what God says about them. The enemy points to every failure as proof that they don't measure up. Be that person that reminds everyone that they are wonderful and amazing because of what God put in them.

You may be the only person to ever mention the good you see in them. People are dying of thirst for lack of encouragement. Let us water their spirits with life coming from our words over them. Let's believe in them until they believe in themselves. Let's go to God for wisdom to see them as He sees them. Let's open our eyes to see what God sees in them even if we may not yet see those things with our eyes. Let's change the world by speaking into others the exact character and being that God placed in them until it becomes visible to everyone. Let's encourage one another as long as it is called today (Hebrews 10:24-25).

To recap on how to greatly increase our love for others:

1. God enjoys telling you what He likes about others.
   a. He knows who He created them to be.
   b. He wants to help us love one another.
2. If you hear/see something bad about people, keep asking God about them – He has more to say.

3. If you are having a hard time hearing something for
    them, either
    a. ask someone else to help you pray or
    b. remind yourself of what the Bible says about
        people.

Additional Resources

Writing things down can be an excellent exercise to help you
remember those things you are learning. Use a journal to
answer the following questions.

1. What are two things God is highlighting for you about
    what was in this chapter?

2. How did Ananias have the courage to speak to Saul?
    How did Peter change his mind about the Gentiles?
    What did Samuel see in Saul to make him king?

3. Think about three people you are serving. Ask God what are some things about them He wants you to know.

4. For those of you who want to dig deeper into this topic, check out these articles:

   - http://prayer-coach.com/0106/friend
   - http://prayer-coach.com/0106/who

7

How to Believe the Best in Others

If you listen to God long enough, you will know He thinks everybody is amazing. The difficulty is that not everyone acts amazingly. Some people consistently make mistakes. Some are often hurtful. And some are just plain dangerous. How are we to believe what God says about them when they may act completely opposite?

What If Their Life Doesn't Match What God Says?

In the last chapter, we saw how Ananias got a view of Saul that was opposite from his experience. Saul became Paul, and Ananias saw a quick turnaround in him (Acts 9:18-21). But what if God shows us things about people and we don't see such a quick turnaround?

Another example we looked was the prophet Samuel's word to a different Saul. He was the man all of Israel hoped for; he was chosen by God to be king. Unfortunately, he made mistakes along the way, and David came along and was also chosen by God to be king.

This is interesting. David didn't see Saul as an obstacle to God's calling on his life. David also didn't reject God's call on Saul's life because of obvious issues, namely Saul trying to kill him. You see, who we are is not defined by what we do, but who we are is exactly who God says we are.

David was running for his life from Saul. A couple times God miraculously intervenes and gave David the opportunity to take Saul's life. David responded by saying "far be it from me to ever lay a hand on the Lord's anointed" (1 Samuel 26:9). Saul was not acting very anointed, but David chose to keep focused on what God said about him, not his actions.

Jesus believed the best of His disciples. He knew that God gave them to Him (John 6:44). He loved them, invested in them, and poured Himself into them. These guys made mistakes. They lacked faith. They wanted to send away kids and adults to whom Jesus wanted to minister (Mark 10:14 & Matthew 14:15). But all of them were there when He wanted to show the full extent of His love – and that included Judas, who betrayed Him.

Jesus knew His Father gave them to Him, and He was going to focus on that view of these guys, and not the behavior they were still showing.

Don't Doubt People's Heart When You Don't Agree

The Apostle Paul had a problem with John Mark. Mark joined Paul and Barnabas on their first missionary journey. Along the way, Mark went back home (Acts 13:13). His departure was hard on Paul, and when it came time for Paul and Barnabas to go on their second journey, Paul refused to go again with Mark, even though Barnabas wanted him (Acts 15:36-41).

The disagreement led to Paul and Barnabas not going together on the next trip. Barnabas took Mark to the same places Mark was a part of in the first journey. Paul joined up with Silas and visited the places on the back half of that same journey that Mark didn't go.

Should Paul and Barnabas have worked out their differences? That's not necessarily the case. It may have been Paul's intense passion for the Gospel that scared Mark away. What I mean is, Mark might not have been the right fit for Paul at that time.

Paul and Barnabas were a successful team, but God could have intentionally used a disagreement about Mark to split them up to double their efforts. I have been a part of many painful disagreements with other believers and friends. These situations at the time moved us in different directions.

Looking back, I can see how God was graciously leading me in a direction that I was not anticipating because of my enjoyment of the relationships were keeping me content. Meaning, because of my love of the friendship, my spiritual antenna was not up to hear God say, "Move". When things became uncomfortable, I was more receptive to hear what God was trying to tell me.

In those difficult situations, it wasn't so much that one or both of us were in the wrong. God wanted to move us in a new direction, but we were unwilling because we loved the friendship.

The point is to fight without becoming critical of the other person. When one or both of you start acting contrary to who you are, step back and ask God what He is doing. Our enemy is always trying to pull you away from others, but at the same time God allows every situation to open us up to hear Him better.

In the end of Paul's life, Paul declared Mark was useful to his work. Even though we are not given the details, reconciliation happened (2 Timothy 4:11). Both men were used by God. We need to look past the hurt we feel in our disagreements with others to see what God is doing.

Sometimes People Are Intentionally Mean

Sometimes the person really is doing bad things. Hitler was a real person, and he did very bad things. There are people who hurt you – and some willingly do it. What should we do? How do we respond?

If we really want to help others, we need to fully believe in the goodness of man. We need to believe that deep down in each person is the greatness that God, Himself, put there. Otherwise, things will get tough with the person we are working with, and we will give up.

There is a maneuver in aviation that is called crabbing. What happens is when there is a strong crosswind during landing that is blowing the plane away from the landing strip, the pilot will turn the craft against the wind so when it gets to the runaway it is actually blown into the place the pilot wanted to go.

We have to see every person with a downward crosswind taking them to become a lesser person than whom God desired. Believing the best in them corrects the trajectory of their life to take them to the destination God had originally designed them for.

Viktor Frankl was a Jewish survivor of the Nazi concentration camps that took the lives of his wife, mother, and brother. He had seen the worst in mankind. Here is his rationale for maintaining a view in man's goodness.

> If we take man as he really is we make him worse. But if we seem to be an idealist and overestimate him, we promote him to what he really can be.[2]

If we presupposed goodness in others, then we will illicit greatness out of them. So when we see people living less than what they could be, we must believe that they are not living out of their true self.

Take for instance a Christian brother or sister who is hurting you or speaking against you in some way. As a Christian, we know that person has the Holy Spirit living in them. The Holy Spirit is there to encourage them to live in accordance with God's plan for their life. Their slander against you is not God's best for them.

So, we can choose to believe that they are an honest, wonderful person, because, that is who the Holy Spirit is working to produce. They are just having trouble making the right choices. Therefore we can either agree with the behavior by equating that to their identity, which we are seeing, or we can agree with the Holy Spirit in who He is creating.

This is where you can use the principles from the previous chapter. Ask Holy Spirit for insight in who He says this person is. Then speak out those things on behalf of the person in prayer or as encouraging words to them.

This is a great tool for a parent. Inevitably your child will go through at least one stage where they pick up behaviors that you as a parent will believe are harmful to them. You can ask the Holy Spirit for this insight into what He is working in your child. Agree with God on these things in prayer. Going to God in this way restores your hope, and your prayers create the spiritual groundwork for your child to respond to the Holy Spirit's leading in his/her life.

Understand that this principle is not only good for Christians. God created each person and has placed greatness in each one. He wants to see everyone reconciled to Him. Therefore anyone who is doing wickedness or evil is not living up to who they were made to be.

Believe In Them Until They Can Believe In Themselves

I went to a seminar on how to help families and individuals hurt by alcoholism[3]. This speaker had worked with alcoholics and their families for over 30 years. He said if he talked to someone for five minutes, God would give him at least three potential amazing destinies for this person. He would then treat this person as if these destinies were going to happen.

People dealing with alcoholism have lost their hope of anything different in their lives. However, when they were around this man, he believed in a better life for them, and it attracted people to him. He believed in them when they couldn't believe in themselves. He continued to believe in them until they started to dare to believe. And, he continued all the more to believe in them until they started living out those better destinies.

Those who have the greatest hope for you will have the biggest influence on your life. Think about your teachers, coaches, or parents that believed in you. They fed your soul because whether they knew it or not, they were speaking the heart of God into you.

We have a chance to be that source of hope for others. The world is trying to tear them down. Their circumstances are trying to agree with the negative life story. The enemy is repeating lies of hopelessness and frustration. You have a chance to stop the downward spiral.

The greatest act of spiritual warfare you may ever do is speaking life into other people.

Let's look at a common example where it is often hard to continue to believe the best: marriage. The following comes from my book Breaking Free[4]:

> Many people with marriage issues face an emotional rollercoaster: good days and bad days. The good days are encouraging, but they are also emotionally draining because you just don't just know when the bad will come. Some days your spouse thinks you are the source of everything wrong; other days they are offering hope to something better.
>
> What is going on? Is your spouse bi-polar? How come you don't know what you are going to get?
>
> On those good days, your spouse is living out of their true self. All of God's works are wonderful therefore when our lives reflect the fruit of the Spirit, we are living out of who God created us to be (Psalm 139:14 and Galatians 5:22). Even if your spouse is not a Christian, deep down God has created in them the desire to have a good and healthy marriage with you.

Since this is God's will for your spouse, the enemy will try to steal, kill, and destroy it (John 10:10). He is feeding lies into your spouse about you, them, and your marriage. Therefore the ups and downs in your marriage are your spouse's choices over which voice they will listen to.

Now before you think this is only a matter of spiritual warfare, your spouse does have responsibility in the matter. And, choices they have made in the past allow the enemy greater influence.

Let's say your spouse had a father that constantly berated them by saying they would never amount to anything. Therefore they grew up with many lies about God and themself. One lie might say God would never come through for them. What happens when there are difficulties in the marriage? The enemy feeds into those lies saying it is not going to work out. God is not going to protect you. You might as well give up. Your spouse is out to get you. They don't believe you will amount to anything anyway. You don't need that kind of pressure.

Because of the events of the past and the lies they already believe, the enemy's lies are now amplified to a degree that they cannot hear the voice of God.

What are you to do? Choose not to respond in like form. When they speak these lies to you, don't get angry. Don't defend yourself. Respond in love. Always proclaim your commitment toward the marriage. In prayer take authority over the enemy reducing his ability to speak to your spouse and to you. As you deny the enemy's ability to speak, then the voice of God will be able to penetrate easier to your spouse. But also don't only focus on the negative; speak out life toward your spouse and the situation. Pronounce the words of God over them and invite more of the presence of God there.

This is not a magic pill. Your spouse still has the choice of whose voice to listen to. But you will be preparing the ground for a better harvest. You can plant the seed, till the ground, and water the plant, but only God can cause it to grow. It is the pleasure of God to change lives. And, even if your spouse decides not to change, God blesses those who choose to give life to others. Rest in His ability to protect and provide for you.

This same perspective can be taken with those that you are trying to serve and help. Ask God what He has to say about the person. Choose to continue to believe it. Speak it to the person as much as they will let you.

You may have a situation like Paul and Barnabas where it is time to go separate ways. Even so, maintain a view of the other person that they are one of God's favorites and pray that they experience every blessing God has in store for them.

Releasing life and blessing over them will help you to be available to continue to give help to others.

Additional Resources

Writing things down can be an excellent exercise to help you remember those things you are learning. Use a journal to answer the following questions.

1. What are two things God is highlighting for you about what was in this chapter?

2. How do we find goodness in seemingly evil people?

3. If there is someone you have a hard time believing the good God says about them, then write down those good things. In prayer, say, "I choose to believe that this person is (fill in the blank with a good quality)." As you regularly do this, you will start to see them in this way.

4. For those of you who want to dig deeper into this topic, check out this article:

    - http://prayer-coach.com/0107/good

8

How to Trust God in the Process

In the last chapter, we looked at how to believe the best in others, especially when they are doing evil. We reviewed three ways to believe the best in others:

1. Ask God for His perspective on the person.
2. Believe God's view over what you see.
3. Believe it for them until they believe it for themselves.

As we are believing the best for others, we may be tempted to move ahead of God. God often gives great and precious promises about people that seem too good to be true (2 Peter 1:4). He does this for us, and He also does it for those we will be serving.

Don't Push Ahead of God

Joseph was just a young boy when he dreamed that his family would serve him one day. In his naiveté, he shared this dream with them, and they developed a strong hatred towards him. Instead of jumping straight into a place of authority over his family, he first spent many years as a slave, followed with many more years in prison before those promises came true.

We often want to hurry along the promises we see for of others by putting them into positions before they are ready. Just as we need to trust God for what He says about others; we also need to trust God for the process to get them there.

King Saul was anointed to be king of Israel. The prophet Samuel declared it would happen and the people of Israel rallied around him. Saul didn't do anything to make it happen; God made him king.

While he wasn't looking for this title, he didn't trust God to continue what He started. Having taken over leadership, Saul started to protect Israel from its enemy, the Philistines. This led to a large military build up near Gilgal. The enemy's number was so large that the Israelites were scared and many fled.

Samuel had told Saul to wait seven days for him. With his troops leaving, Saul decided to take things in his own hands. He prepares the sacrifice in hopes it would build confidence in his army. Samuel arrived as Saul finished preparing the offering.

Overstepping his role, Saul forfeited future blessings from God. Saul remained king the rest of his life, but he forfeited a blessing God had in store for him which was that his children would follow him as kings (1 Samuel 13:13-14). Saul doubted God's process and lost the greater blessing that was in store.

God remained true to what He promised Saul, but there would have been more if only He would have trusted in the process.

Now David was also promised to be king over Israel. There were times where it looked as if God was making it happen. The people started acknowledging him as a leader – "Saul has killed his thousands; David has killed his tens of thousands" (1 Samuel 18:7). Even though Saul was trying to kill David, David appeared to have two opportunities to take Saul's life but didn't (1 Samuel 24:4-7 & 26:5-8).

David made mistakes in the waiting, but he never forced the promises to come to pass. He believed them. He held onto them. But he waited for God to make them happen.

It wasn't an easy process. Saul was chasing him around trying to kill him, he was living in caves, and he was waiting on God to transition him to be king. We read about some of what He was feeling in the Psalms. This is from Psalm 59:1-10, written when Saul had sent men to watch over David's house in order to kill him.

1   Deliver me from my enemies, O God;
    be my fortress against those who are attacking me.
2   Deliver me from evildoers
    and save me from those who are after my blood.
3   See how they lie in wait for me!
    Fierce men conspire against me
    for no offense or sin of mine, Lord.
4   I have done no wrong, yet they are ready to attack me.

Arise to help me; look on my plight!
5   You, Lord God Almighty,
    you who are the God of Israel,
    rouse yourself to punish all the nations;
    show no mercy to wicked traitors.
6   They return at evening,
    snarling like dogs,
    and prowl about the city.
7   See what they spew from their mouths—
    the words from their lips are sharp as swords,
    and they think, "Who can hear us?"
8   But you laugh at them, Lord;
    you scoff at all those nations.
9   You are my strength, I watch for you;
    you, God, are my fortress,
10 my God on whom I can rely.

God wants us to trust in Him. It's easy to trust His promises to us when they come right away. Will we continue to hold unto God when He takes a detour to the promise?

God Knows What He Is Doing

Abraham, the father of our faith, knew all about the struggles to trust God's process. He was 75 years old when God promised that he would be a great nation. Ten years later Abraham and Sarah were still without a child. The process was getting long, and Abraham and Sarah were getting old. That is when they took the detour and decided their servant Hagar would have a child in Sarah's place.

Ishmael was born. Everything was now clicking along the promise. It just seemed God needed some help. The only problem was that Ishmael was not the promised son.

The process of God more than likely will not follow the path that we think. Will we still continue trusting God?

When Joshua entered into the Promised Land, he was overwhelmed by the task of going against Jericho. He knew that was the correct path, but he was also aware of how great the task was. Jericho seemed unbeatable. He sought God's direction for the battle and found a most unusual battle plan.

Joshua 6 tells the story. They had to walk around the city for several days without saying a word. Finally on the last day they gave a great shout and the city was overtaken. This is wonderful – God was with them to help them take the Promised Land.

However, as the Israelites moved on from there to take on the city of Ai, this time they didn't seek the Lord, as it appeared something they could handle themselves. They were wrong and suffered a major defeat, which melted the hearts of the Israelites. How could God let this happen?

They sought the Lord and find out there was sin in the camp. God wanted that dealt with before moving forward. They did that, and God gave them another specific plan. They won, and everyone was happy again.

That is, everyone but their enemies. One group of people decided they needed to trick the Israelites otherwise they would be destroyed. The Gibeonites pretend to be a far off nation in order to get the Israelites to sign a treaty with them.

The Israelites heard their story, checked their provisions, and agreed to protect them. After the delegation from Gibeon left, the Israelites realized they were deceived.

The neighboring nations were upset the Gibeonites sided with their enemies and conspired together to destroy Gibeon. Gibeon called out for help from Israel. Frustrated that they had been tricked, Israel went to God to decide what they should do.

God wanted them to honor their agreement, even though it shouldn't have been made, and gave them the plan for battle.

The point of this history lesson is that the Israelites knew the promise. They were to take the land. However, they still needed to seek God for the process. Several times the promise seemed to be in jeopardy, but going to God brought them back on track.

As we help people, we may not see those we are working with moving toward the expected promise. At times we may feel that everything is going in the wrong direction. We need to hold onto what God has shown us.

We should ask God how we are to move forward, but we might find His reply doesn't make sense. God's ways are not like ours (Isaiah 55:8-9). He moves us into directions that challenge what makes sense to us and calls us into greater dependence on Him.

Unless We See From God's Perspective, His Ways Don't Make Sense

Think through Jesus' life on earth. Even though He was God, He lived His time on earth as a man. He didn't stop being God, but He limited some of His abilities, such as His ability to know everything and be everywhere. He said He only did what He saw the Father doing and only spoke what He heard the Father saying (John 5:19; 12:49).

And, His ability to see and hear the Father was no greater than our ability to see or hear Him. If we can agree to this, then we must believe that His need to have faith was also just as necessary as ours. To some degree, He needed to trust what He heard and saw were from God and He needed to trust that God would follow through with what He said He would do. When Jesus told the storm to be still, there was some level of faith that said, "God, you are going to have to come through here" (Matthew 8:26).

With that in mind, when Jesus went to the cross, it could only make sense by keeping His focus on the Father. Jesus' ability to rise from the dead was not in His power to do. He had to trust the Father to raise Him. Seeing it from this viewpoint makes

Jesus' prayer at Gethsemane more understandable – He was realigning His faith that the cross was the path to bring us back to God.

If we try to make sense of what God calls us to do, we will limit what He wants to do through us. We can't let circumstances guide us. We can't let our feelings lead us. Miracles never make sense unless we see our situation from God's viewpoint.

You can't make the promise happen. That is how you end up with an Ishmael instead of an Isaac (Galatians 4:23). The fruit of your effort will never inherit the promise (Galatians 4:30). God's promises are reserved for the fruit of His labor through you.

God Wants You To Receive The Promise More Than You Do

When my family got to China to help teenage orphan girls, we had in mind that we would get a farm to give us space to take care of them. Early on, our daughter had a dream that a foreigner would give us the farm. In the dream, the farm had a three-story house on it, a lot of fruit trees, water in front, and many dogs. The dream also said that the foreigner would give us 10%.

We held onto this dream. We believed it was from God, but there were plenty of things we didn't understand. For one, we didn't know foreigners could own land in China. Secondly, we wondered what we could do with this information. Should we go up to foreigners, ask them if they have a farm, and then ask them if they would give it to us?

A year and a half after our daughter had this dream, an intern with us was talking to a foreigner in our city. This man asked our intern what he was doing. He said he was working with Kevin and Allison, who hoped to get a farm to help teenage orphan girls. This man instantly responded, "I have a farm; you can have it."

He gave us 10 acres of his 100-acre farm. This farm has a three-story house, thousands of peach trees, a lake in front, and several dogs. It was incredible; we knew it was from God. It's a story we hold onto knowing God will make the greater dream of helping teenage orphan girls happen.

Sometimes we have to be willing to appear foolish. We need to be willing to be hurt. We need to be willing to let everything die, and trust God to take care of everything. We may never understand the outcome, but God says He rewards those who have faith (Hebrews 11:6). He wants us to trust Him in the process.

Here are three steps for you to trust in God in the process:

1. Remind yourself that God is trustworthy. He is faithful and rewards those who trust in Him.
2. When things appear to be moving away from the promise, ask God if there is some new direction He has for you to move you to the promise.

3. Go back and redo step 1. God wants you to achieve your promise more than you do.

Additional Resources

Writing things down can be an excellent exercise to help you remember those things you are learning. Use a journal to answer the following questions.

1. What are two things God is highlighting for you about what was in this chapter?

2. Is there an area you find it more difficult to trust God? How can you grow your trust?

3. Think about someone you are serving who is not living out of the goodness God has put in them. Ask God if there is another way you can water growth in them.

4. For those of you who want to dig deeper into this topic, check out this article:

   • http://prayer-coach.com/0108/faith

9

How Not to Burnout

The greatest risk of being a caregiver is the potential of burning out. We long for others to get better, to feel loved, and to have their needs met. We serve them, pray for them, and give our attention to them. We can become so focused on others that we forget to pay attention to our own needs. God says that He will take care of our every need, but if we are constantly ignoring our own needs, we will also ignore His provisions for those needs. That is the pathway to burnout.

If you want to go into a field that helps others, you have to realize that you will have a never-ending supply of patients that will look to you as their savior. You will be pushed to the end of yourself as you see the depths of hurt and loss that people will look to you to fix.

Statistics on Burnout

In a 2010 study that appeared in Psychology Today[5], it stated 10 careers with the highest rates of depression. Nursing topped the list. Others on the list were social workers, other health care workers, and teachers. These people constantly give of themselves with little feedback or recognition of their selfless giving.

Ministry did not make the list, so we may be tempted to think that Christians can handle the stress better. But, according to a 2006 study conducted by Dr. Richard J. Krejcir[6]:

- 90% of pastors surveyed stated they are frequently fatigued and worn out on a weekly or even daily basis.
- 77% ... felt they did not have a good marriage.
- 75% ... felt they were unqualified and/or poorly trained by their seminaries to lead and manage the church or to counsel others. This left them disheartened in their ability to pastor.
- 71% ... constantly fight depression
- 70% ... do not have close friends

A 2007 study by the Schaeffer Institute of Church Leadership Development[7] showed 70 percent of pastors were so stressed that they would regularly consider leaving the ministry. As our Christian leaders, we assume they would have the tools to maintain effectiveness in ministry, and yet the average person is doing better with overall happiness. As we head into a helps profession, we have to realize that this pressure is real.

If we naively press on thinking Jesus will take care of us, we will have to assume that we have figured out something that 90% of pastors didn't. The tools put together for you in the

Academy of Powerful Caregivers is designed to help you get there, but don't assume the battle is not real.

Recently, a megachurch pastor from America just stepped down and left the ministry. It doesn't matter who it was because whenever you are reading this, there will be another story just as similar. This particular man started the church 7 years ago and stated as he was stepping down that he wasn't doing well and hasn't been for some time. In his words, he was "tired and broken."

If this was your pastor and you were on the leadership team with him, what would you say? What would you encourage him to do? How would you counsel him?

Would you pray with him? Help him connect with God, so he could stay on as the pastor? Would you wonder if he was secretly in sin?

The leaders of his church did try to talk him into staying. The pastor offered to be available to answer whatever questions that came up about the church, of which they definitively declared they would take advantage.

What did this man need? Did he need to hear that they didn't know how to move on without him? Did he need their pleas to get him to stay? When people are teetering on burnout, what do they need from us?

What Did Moses Need to Protect Him From Burnout?

After the Israelites escaped from Egypt and were getting settled into life in the desert, Moses was inadvertently preparing himself for burnout. He was trying to lead a nation and handle every single problem himself. Moses would sit between each disagreement in order to give God's desires and decrees (Exodus 18:13-17). His heart for the people was going to wear him out.

His father-in-law came to see him. He rejoiced hearing the stories of all that God had done, he worship God together with Moses, and watched how things were going now. He saw Moses working from morning to evening managing every issue the people had. Finally, he told Moses he was doing too much and he was going to wear himself out (Exodus 18:18).

Here is the help Moses received from his father-in-law:

1. **He addressed the problem.** Many of us don't know we are headed for burnout. We think this is our calling that we need to persevere.
2. **He gave Moses permission to not do it all.** When it's our calling and we see a need, we move to do it. We need to be wise and pray through which things will have the greatest impact.
3. **He encouraged Moses to get help.** The hardest part of someone who has a calling is realizing that part of your role is to rise up other leaders to help you accomplish the task.

I believe this is what the megachurch pastor we referenced earlier needed to hear. But, this is not just an issue with pastors. As I already mentioned, depression is a common affliction in any occupation that serves others, which is each one of you. This is not to scare any of you, but we need to be aware of this danger.

Case Study on Burnout

Nurses are required to maintain a level of continuing education to keep current in their profession. Courses on burnout are part of that curriculum.

Here is what a typical case study from one of those courses would look like:

Laura, a nurse who works in an assisted living facility, gives medications, provides wound care, writes care plans, maintains patient records, and more.

At first, Laura felt challenged and proud of her ability to manage so many responsibilities. Then one attendant went on maternity leave and another quit, leaving her normal shift extremely short-staffed. Laura again loved the challenge and assumed the responsibilities of the others who left. She thought it would only be for a few days or weeks. Soon, she felt her kindness of helping out became an expectation to cover the workload of three people.

As this continued for some weeks, Laura became more and more tired, frustrated, and angry. Then, one day, she made an error with a patient's medication. Fortunately, the person was not harmed, but the physician on duty confronted her in front of other staff members.

Ashamed, Laura lost confidence and began to think of herself as a failure. She even started to question her decision to become a nurse. As her self-doubt increased, she began distancing herself from her coworkers, friends, and family.

At the end of herself, she quit her job, frustrated with the entire healthcare system.

Laura's case illustrates how burnout can creep in. By assuming the extra work of her missing coworkers, Laura became overrun with stress. That caused her job performance to decrease, which increased her feelings of shame and a sense of failure. Ultimately, she quit her job.

WebMD defines "caregiver burnout" as a state of physical, emotional, and mental exhaustion that may be accompanied by a change in attitude -- from positive and caring to negative and unconcerned. Burnout can occur...

- when caregivers don't get the help they need,
- or if they try to do more than they are able -- either physically or financially. Caregivers who are "burned

out" may experience fatigue, stress, anxiety, and depression[8].

Many caregivers also feel guilty if they spend time on themselves rather than on those they are caring for. Taking a break becomes a luxury that seems irresponsible when so many people have "real needs."

Negative job performance is not the only cause of this overload of stress. Remember the megachurch pastor was by all outward appearances successful. Burnout is caused by taking on more than you were meant to carry.

Biblical Example of Burnout

Elijah was an amazing man of God. He was one of the rare men of the Old Testament that regularly walked in miracles. For three years it didn't rain in Israel because Elijah prayed that the rain would stop. During this drought brought on by his prayers, God sent him to a brook for water and sent ravens to feed him. When the brook dried up, God sent Moses to a poor widow. Her flour and oil supernaturally never ran out thus providing food for them. During this time the woman's son died. Elijah prayed and returned him back to his mother alive (1 Kings 17:1 -24).

Elijah was walking in miraculous provisions from God. When it came time for the rain to return, Elijah challenged Ahab to gather all of his prophets of Baal for a challenge at Mt. Carmel. Before those 450 pagan prophets, the fire of God fell from heaven to accept Elijah's sacrifice. The people of Israel turned on these false prophets and struck them down (1 Kings 18:16-20).

I want you to see that there was incredible favor on Elijah. God was with Elijah no matter what he did. You need to understand this to understand that burnout is real.

Ahab told Jezebel what Elijah had done, and she demanded that Elijah would be put to death for his actions. Elijah became so scared that he ran for his life. Please realize this was nothing new; she had already been trying to kill him. This time, however, Elijah ran and prayed that God would end his misery and just take his life (1 Kings 19:4).

God gave him some rest, food, and water. Then God instructed him to go to Horeb, about a 40-day journey. Having arrived, God asked Elijah what was wrong. Elijah told God how he was so devoted to Him and all the other Israelites were not. He was the only one trying to serve Him, and now they were trying to kill him (1 Kings 19:10).

Remember the stats we started with? Most pastors feel frequently fatigued, regularly depressed, and have no close friends. Could Elijah fall into this category?

How did God help Elijah? Did He let Elijah hide out alone at Mt. Horeb until he felt better? Did God give Elijah more important work? Did God strike down Ahab and Jezebel? Did He have all the Israelites repent? NO!

God let Elijah know he wasn't alone, and then God sent Elijah to go be with people.

People Protect Us From Burnout

In the beginning, God said it is not good for man to be alone (Genesis 2:18). And what was God's solution to man's problem? Did He give us more of Himself? No. He gave us other people.

The apostle Paul understood this. Every letter is filled with personal greetings to friends he made in his travels or sending friends along with the correspondence.

In 2 Timothy 4, Paul shares about a particularly hard time. Someone strongly opposed Paul, and everyone deserted him. Paul acknowledged how God protected him, strengthened him, and stood by his side. While Paul acknowledged all that God had done, he now wanted friends. He asks Timothy to come quickly to him and to also send Mark along (2 Timothy 4:9-18).

Paul was at a crucial time where it would have been easy to fall into depression. Like Elijah, Paul was experiencing separation from others but also experiencing God coming through for him. Paul, likely being in a Roman prison, was creating a safety net by requesting friends to come to him.

Burnout can hit the best of us. In fact, research suggests that the best caregivers – those detail-oriented, perfectionistic, deeply compassionate souls among us – are at the highest risk of burnout.

Why? Because the realities of the job "don't always match up to their high standards, and the resulting stress and frustration, over time, leads the physical and mental exhaustion that's characteristic of burnout.[9]" (Nursing Link)

How do we avoid burnout?

1. Find hobbies you enjoy and make time for them.
2. Spend time with God... not just getting material for work.
3. Don't allow what you are doing become who you are.
4. Remind yourself of all the good things God has done for you. Thanksgiving is a vehicle to take you to joy, which is an attitude you can choose.
5. Cultivate relationships with people who know you well. Let them into your mind and heart. You need people who will accept you even if you feel awful.
6. Have your friends remind you of the things God placed in you and the good things He has done for you (repeating steps 3 & 4).

The next chapter will be about relationships. How do we develop those types of friends that will accept us and push us to God? That chapter will help you implement the fifth and sixth step in the path away from burnout.

Additional Resources

Writing things down can be an excellent exercise to help you remember those things you are learning. Use a journal to answer the following questions.

1. What are two things God is highlighting for you about what was in this chapter?

2. What are some ways other people help us avoid burnout?

3. Name three people you would like to maintain as close friends. Talk to each one this week sharing something personal with them.

4. For those of you who want to dig deeper into this topic, check out this article:

- http://prayer-coach.com/0109/joy

10

How Relationships Can Help You

In the last chapter, we looked at how to avoid burnout and how people in our profession are vulnerable to it. In particular, we looked at how having close friends can protect you from burning out. We need people who will accept us even if we feel awful. This step is very important to maintaining our longevity and health.

Friends Invest Into You

As we saw in the Krejcir study[10]:

- 70% of pastors surveyed stated they do not have close friends.

As people who love God, you will always have others in your life who are going through struggles and looking to you as a sounding board and listening ear. It is a way we can express to them our kind and compassionate heavenly Father. God sends people to us, so we can show them that they are important and valued.

Because of their pain, often these people are needy and only focused on themselves and their issues. We are to minister love to them because they are important, but we can't conclude that they are our close friends just because they want to spend time with us. They are valuing what we give to them, not investing into who we are. That kind of relationship will only lead to hinder our view of ourselves.

It is easy as lovers of people to get so focused on helping others that we forget that we also are important. When you surround yourself with people who only talk about themselves and never ask about you, your life becomes focused solely on others.

Not acknowledging what is going on with you, leads you to think you are not important. By not sharing about yourself, you are not allowing yourself to find people interested in you. You don't want to focus solely on yourself, but neither should your friends think only of themselves... if they are to be friends.

God created you because He thought you were important. He knew you would bring something of value to His world. We need friends that will draw those treasures out of us.

Friends want what is best for each other. You will want to minister to your friends by reminding them of who they are, what they can do, and by rejoicing or crying with them. True friends will do the same for you.

How Do We Find Friends?

The Old Testament tells a wonderful story of friendship through the man after God's heart and his soul mate, Jonathan.

If you remember, David raised his hand and volunteered to fight the Philistine, Goliath. God worked a miracle, and David took him out with a sling and a stone. David cut off Goliath's head and then chased the rest of the Philistine army with the head in his hand.

Saul turned to his commander and asked who David was. Nobody knew, so when David came back, the commander brought him to Saul. David told his story to Saul in the presence of Saul's son, Jonathan. Having heard David speak, Jonathan became one in spirit with him (1 Samuel 17:55 - 18:1).

Jonathan also loved the Lord and had tasted of what it was like to have God come on him in power. Jonathan had taken his armor bearer up into the Philistine camp, two against an entire army, and he trusted God's provision of handing Israel's enemies over to them (1 Samuel 14:1-15). So, when he heard David's faith, Jonathan knew he found someone who could understand him and someone he wanted to be near. In an instant, the Bible says Jonathan loved David as himself. And we know that David also loved Jonathan.

These two men found a kindred spirit between them. They loved God and believed He would act on their behalf. And, they knew that they became more alive by being together. Those things God sparked in their hearts were fanned into flame in the other's presence. Friends are made to do that for you. They are to awaken God's spirit within you and call out the desires God placed there.

Who Can Really Understand Me?

The problem we have as caretakers is that we see and hear things that are difficult to let other people into. How many people in the health care profession have had to watch someone die? You may work with the elderly and you daily see some of them abandoned by their kids and left to finish off their days alone. Pastors hear people share how their husband or wife left them for someone else. If you work at shelters, you hear about women who have been raped, beaten by husbands, and left to take care of their kids alone. The list goes on and on.

It's hard to find friends who will understand what we go through. Most people live in their safe world, unexposed to its evils. A lot of what we experience, we can't tell anyone else. Most of the time, we don't even tell our spouses the load we are carrying.

Another finding of that same Krejcir study[11] stated:

- 77% of pastors surveyed stated they do not have a good marriage.

This is unhealthy. Remember, God said it was not good for man to be alone. We were all born into a family, and when we became Christians, we were again placed into a family. We need each other.

There are around 45 verses with commands about how we are to treat one another. Many of them are to love one another and encourage one another. While it is important that we do this, let's also remember we need to allow people to do this to us. We need to allow some people to bear our burdens, have fellowship with us, and serve our needs. We need to find friends.

Friends Call Out Your Identity

God created us and placed within each of us a unique way to express God to this world. We are each amazing because God made us (Psalm 139:14). However, most of us never live out of who God made us to be. We are either embarrassed by our weaknesses or fearful that people will think we are prideful for expressing our strengths. Therefore we live in this lukewarm middle, barely expressing the full nature of what God put in us.

Friends help us live out of who we are because as we are ourselves with them, their acceptance of us allows us to believe in God's acceptance of us. We can see the eyes of God's love best through the eyes of one another.

We may understand this as a mental agreement, but there is more behind it. The more we hide from one another about ourselves, the more we will hide from God. And, the more we hide from God, the less we will hear from Him. Since He talks to who we are created to be, if we hide areas from Him, we turn off ways He wants to speak to us.

Many of the people we will help are suffering because they are scared of people. Most of our hurt has come through relationships. However, the more we hide, the less we get healed and the less we ask for help. The more we feel alone with our problems, the greater the burden they become to us.

We know this for others, but we seem to forget this for ourselves. The enemy of our souls wants to come in and isolate us from others. He pushes us into unforgiveness and hatred. He makes us afraid of what others may think, say, or do. He knows if he can get you isolated, you will be vulnerable to his lies.

Notice what Adam and Eve did when they sinned. They hid (Genesis 3:8). God responded by providing a way for them get back into fellowship. They felt they were naked, so God made them clothes. God is always trying to bring us back into relationship.

Whatever we hide from relationship highlights a breakdown of trust. Some people may not be safe to go there with us, but God has given you some people that can handle your mess. Until we see other people accept us in our mess, we will never come out of the pressure to perform for acceptance.

We Can't Lead Others Into Vulnerability If We Don't Go There

I need to come back to this point: it isn't only our sin that we are hiding from people. There are plenty of things that aren't sins that we hide. We may think we are not smart, so we hide behind being quiet. We may think we are ugly, so we hide underneath baggy clothing. We may think our dreams are too big and prideful, so we hide behind acceptable goals.

God created you, so you are smart, beautiful, and worthy of outrageous goals. As we find people we can talk to about these things, we will stop blocking God's purposes for our lives.

In order to come out of hiding, we will need to take risks with our friends. When we share those secret places from within us, we won't know how they are going to respond. But, we need to take the risk. Keeping them hidden limits us to what we will allow God to do. Hiding creates a protective cover to the lies we believe and keeps us from living in all God has for us.

I believe you are already providing safe places for other people to share what is going on in their hearts. You desire to see people become all God created them to be. You want to remove the lies they think about themselves in order to see themselves as loved by God.

Allow others to be that person to you. We will have a hard time expecting others to be vulnerable if we are not vulnerable ourselves.

As I mentioned before, David and Jonathan became friends. The story continues with Jonathan's dad, King Saul, becoming very jealous of David. After running away, David finds Jonathan to ask what he has done. This seemingly simple question is a risk for David because it is about Jonathan's dad. Jonathan denies his father's intentions of killing David, but then David doubles down by declaring on oath it was true.

Sometimes you have to risk losing your friendship in order to protect it. You may think your friend can't handle a certain part of you, so you hold back. As soon as you shut people out, you start killing the relationship. By holding back, you don't even allow them to become the friend you once thought they were.

David takes that risk and strengthens his friendship. When Jonathan confirms his father's desire to kill David, he reestablishes his devotion to David. That thing that you fear will cause rejection is actually the path to deeper friendship. Our fears in relationships are only overcome by taking the risk to be vulnerable.

Friends Help Us Relate To God

Why is friendship so important? Because it teaches us how to be friends with God. God is looking for these kinds of friends who will expose their hearts to Him and will listen when He exposes His heart.

God will always listen to you, remind you of how valuable you are, and allow you to take the spotlight. But, will we do this for God? Will we listen to His heart or will we only tell Him what is going on with us? He wants us to be His friends.

Look for true friends in your life because God has them available for you. Become true friends to others, and it will draw more people to you. Develop your friendship with God because that is what you were created for.

The next chapter will be more about this friendship with God.

Additional Resources

Writing things down can be an excellent exercise to help you remember those things you are learning. Use a journal to answer the following questions.

1. What are two things God is highlighting for you about what was in this chapter?

2. What are some benefits of having friends?

3. Think about 2 friends you have. What is something you can do this week to develop a closer relationship with them?

4. For those of you who want to dig deeper into this topic, check out this article:

    •   http://prayer-coach.com/0110/risks

11

How to Pursue God

As powerful caregivers, we need to cultivate intimate relationships. They protect us from burnout and help us maintain the passion of our calling for the longevity of our lives. Here are some benefits we discussed in the last chapter:

1. We understand God's acceptance through the acceptance of others.
2. Even though relationships have caused us pain, relationships are where we will find healing.
3. We don't believe our value if we are afraid to share ourselves with others.
4. Relationships push us to become all God created us to be.
5. Relationships with others teach us how to have a friendship with God.

This last point leads us into this chapter's topic: friendship with God.

Can We Really Know A Holy God?

Historically, friendship with God has been a taboo. When Jesus talked of God as His Father, He was nearly killed. As followers of God, we desire to maintain God's holiness and purity by limiting our access to Him.

We may want to witness to others to get them to believe in Jesus, but we feel the need to press home their sinfulness and separation from God. When people do trust in Jesus for their salvation, we teach that they enter a sanctification process of slowly working out their sin. They may get better and better, but any sin that lingers is enough to cause a significant separation between them and God.

Jesus is different. We accept His closeness. The Holy Spirit really just confuses us, but we will accept that He is near and helping. God, the heavenly Father, however, is sitting distantly on His throne. We can talk to Him in prayer, but actual closeness has to be reserved for when we get to heaven.

I was at a large conference where a famous Christian speaker was giving a series of talks. He shared how he heard someone say that God would spend time with him each morning when he was shaving. This speaker quipped, "Did he keep on shaving?" Everybody laughed.

The point he went on to make is that if God shows up, you'd better fall to your knees because His holiness could strike you dead.

That's not really the kind of God that you want to spend time with. How can you boldly come before His throne if you are fearful He will strike you down (Hebrews 4:16)? Jesus portrayed a different view of the Father.

Jesus best describes the Father in the parable of the Prodigal Son. When this son returns from his hedonistic lifestyle, we don't see a holy father keeping his distance. Instead, we see the father running to the son before there was even a confession and giving him hugs and kisses (Luke 15:20).

Jesus Made A Way For Us

When Jesus went to the cross, He removed the barriers that kept us from God.

What about the verse that suggests that Jesus is our revelation of the Father? It seems to show that since God is too holy for us, we only need look at Jesus to see the Father (John 14:6-9).

Jesus states that He is the only way to the Father and that if you know Him, you will know the Father as well. Philip desiring more of God asks Jesus to show them the Father because that would be enough for them. Jesus' response was, "Don't you know Me? If you have seen me, you have seen the Father. How can you ask this (John 14:9)?" The point wasn't you can't see the Father; the point was you should have already been seeing Him!

Yes, when we see Jesus, we have seen the Father. But that is not all we get to do. No one can come to the Father but through Jesus, which means that we can actually come to the Father.

Hebrews encourages us to boldly come to the Father's throne of grace (Hebrews 4:16). Hebrews and James both encourage us to draw near to Him (Hebrews 10:22 & James 4:6).

We may see ourselves as unimportant or think God is too holy, but these are just lies from the enemy to keep God's treasure (you) away from Him. Do you know what Jesus' reward was for His suffering? It was to bring you and me into the presence of God (1 Peter 3:18). To deny your ability to come to God is to either state your lack of faith in Jesus' atonement for you or to belittle the work of the cross that tore down your alienation from God.

We can theorize about whether God wants us to come to Him or whether we have the ability, but it is most assuredly not going to happen if we don't start to seek Him. Let's make a decisive effort to seek God's face (Psalm 27:8). This will take time set aside from other things. It will require actively being still and focusing our minds on Him.

Abraham Shows Us How To Be God's Friend

The Bible calls Abraham a friend of God (Isaiah 41:8 & James 2:23). And, we can learn a lot about coming to God by looking at his life.

The first thing we see in their friendship is that they made promises to each other. We know that God spoke to Abraham saying that He would bless him and those who bless him and curse those that curse him (Genesis 12:2-3). We are told God promised him land in Canaan and many offspring (Genesis 13:14-17). But we see when Abraham came back from fighting the five kings, he had made a promise to God not to take anything from others so they couldn't claim they made him rich (Genesis 14:22-23).

The second thing is Abraham believed God's promises. When God told him to go to a place He would show him, Abraham went. When God told him he would have offspring, Abraham believed him. As you read the account in Genesis, it seems that Abraham's belief in God's promises made room for God to promise even more to Abraham.

This was extremely evident when God asked Abraham to kill his only son, Isaac. Abraham moved forward in faith, rationalizing that God would raise Isaac from the dead (Hebrews 11:17-19). Friends trust one another.

God, in turn, gave Abraham wealth. He seemed to succeed in everything he did. God took care of Abraham. God protected him. Friends look after each other.

God also overlooked Abraham's mistakes. Because Abraham valued his friendship with God and never turned to other gods, when he did show lack of trust, God continued to bless and protect him. Twice Abraham lied and put his wife, Sarah, in danger, but God protected them (Genesis 12:13, 17-20, 20:2-3).

As we already spoke about, Abraham also wavered in his faith and tried to make the promise happen through his wife's maidservant, Hagar. God guided Abraham through this time, but God still blessed Ishmael because of his friendship with Abraham (Genesis 21:11-13).

God visited Abraham often. The Bible is unclear how this started or how it was maintained. It is just written as a matter of fact. God spoke to Abraham. This could have been an audible voice or a voice in his head. Whatever the case, Abraham believed it was from God. Abraham knew there was something to it, and he believed. Sometimes God's words to Abraham appear to be a phrase or a few promises (Genesis 12:2-3). Other times they appear to be long conversations (Genesis 17).

It would have been nice if the Bible gave us a practical guide for how Abraham recognized God speaking to him. On the other hand, if we were given that guide, we would make that the only way God would speak, and it seems God likes to use many different ways to speak to us. Sometimes it is through dreams. Sometimes visions. Sometimes impressions. Sometimes through other people. And, sometimes as other people.

Genesis 18 is the account of three men walking past Abraham's land. Abraham sees them and requests that they take a rest and allow him to serve them. These men turn out to be from the Lord. In this encounter, they confirmed God's promise to Abraham that the heir would come through Sarah. Then God did another thing that confirms Abraham as friend: God confided in him (Genesis 18:17).

The Lord told Abraham His intent to see the wickedness of Sodom and Gomorrah. Abraham knew this meant the potential destruction of those cities. Then Abraham did something astounding – he tried to talk God out of it.

True friendship is not one-sided. We often think that we need to try to hear from God and then do whatever He says. We feel we should be robots, slaves, or soldiers following through with the commands of the Lord. God really wants us to be friends. He tells us what He is going to do, so we can start having His mind about things.

Questioning God is not dishonoring Him as long as it is out of love for Him. Abraham knew how to obey when he didn't want to and when it didn't make sense (e.g. trying to kill Isaac). However, we can as a friend ask Him questions.

Jesus calls us friends and defines it as making everything from the Father known to us. He doesn't want to keep us in the dark (John 15:15). He wants to bring us into the process.

Abraham loved God for God's sake and followed Him fully. And so, the Lord made him His confidant and found pleasure in manifesting Himself to him and in trusting to him His sacred promises. Here are the examples we see that show Abraham is a friend of God:

1.   Promises were made to each other.
2.   Abraham believed God to fulfill His promises.
3.   They trusted each other (Isaac).
4.   God blessed Abraham.
5.   God overlooked his offenses.
6.   The Lord visited Abraham often.
7.   God disclosed secrets to Abraham.
8.   Abraham shared his thoughts with God.

Abraham was an amazing character in the Bible. He is the father of our faith. He revolutionized how we can connect with God. But, he is not intended to be an abnormality. The heroes of the faith in the Bible are highlighted to draw us into greater depths with God. They show us what can be accomplished and encourage us to go even deeper.

The same can be said for Jesus' earthly ministry. He walked in extreme closeness with God, but it wasn't because He was God. He showed us how we can do it in our humanity. We can do even greater things than Jesus (John 14:12).

How are we to accomplish these same results? Well, that is going to look different for each of us. Let me just lay out what drawing closer to God is not.

1. Drawing near to God is not magic.
2. Drawing near to God is not presenting your prayer list.
3. Drawing near to God is not getting material for your ministry.
4. Drawing near to God does not manipulate Him to act on your behalf.
5. Drawing near to God does not force Him to answer you more quickly.
6. Drawing near to God does not prove yourself to Him.
7. Drawing near to God does not make your problems go away.
8. Drawing near to God does not make you better than other people.

Drawing near to God is an attitude of the mind and heart (Colossians 3:1-3). It is spending time in relationship with our Creator. To some degree, each of the things listed in the previous list may happen, but that is not the focus. Drawing near is a lifestyle of living in relationship with God.

Ultimately, drawing near to God is a personal and private time with God. You are not necessarily meant to share everything from those times. It is a private kingdom that you protect and treasure. You may at times feel released to share from those times with Him, but that should not be expected.

God loves you. Jesus came to bring you to God (1 Peter 3:18). We have been reconciled with God (2 Corinthians 5:18-20). He intends us to draw near.

Additional Resources

Writing things down can be an excellent exercise to help you remember those things you are learning. Use a journal to answer the following questions.

1. What are two things God is highlighting for you about what was in this chapter?

2. What aspects of Abraham's friendship with God do you relate with most?
   Which ones do you relate with the least? Why?

3. Why can we approach God's throne with confidence (Hebrews 4:16)?
   Are there times when you feel less confident?
   How can you hold firmly to the faith you possess (Hebrews 4:14)?

4. For those of you who want to dig deeper into this topic, check out these resources:

   • http://prayer-coach.com/0111/live
   • http://prayer-coach.com/0111/qt
   • http://prayer-coach.com/0111/song

12

How to Convince Yourself that Powerful Caregivers Flow from Love

Throughout this book, I have given you plenty of opportunities to write down your thoughts. I know that we only retain a portion of what we read. Writing engages us with the material to show us what we really believe and transform what we think about God, ourselves, and being a powerful caregiver. The goal of this book is not to give material; it is to release life into all of your work. I believe God wants each of you to be powerful caregivers.

For those wanting the certificate of completion for this material, there is a requirement of writing a theme paper. However, everyone is welcome to participate. Each module of this series has a theme. For the Module 1: The Motivation of a Caregiver, the theme is "All powerful caregivers flow in love."

Here are the requirements of the paper:

PAPER: Theme: All powerful caregivers flow in love.

Step 1: Answer each of the following questions:

→ What biblical foundation have you found for believing this theme? Please give at least one Old and one New Testament example.

→ Do you see anyone in Scripture possessing a belief in this theme? If so, what impact did the belief have on his or her life?

→ Where do you see this theme in the life of Jesus and what impact did it have in His life?

→ Scripturally, are there any instructions given on how to live this theme out? Explain.

Step 2: Choose ONLY 1 or 2 of the following questions as part of Step 2

→ What difference has this theme made in your life?

→ Were you surprised by what you found in Scripture? Why? What did you learn?

→ In what ways do you actively apply this theme to your life?

→ What challenges have you faced and overcome in living out this theme?

→ How has this theme changed the way you think?

→ What testimony in your life demonstrates or has demonstrated the power of this theme?

→ What key experiences or learning moments have helped you integrate this theme into your lifestyle? (ex: Scripture, literature, messages, declarations, testimonies, personal or corporate encounters etc.)

Step 3: Choose ONLY 1 or 2 of the following questions as part of Step 3

→ Looking forward after this course, how will living from this theme change how you interact with yourself and others (especially when in a caregiver role)?

→ Are there any changes you need to make in your life to line up with this theme at a deeper level? What are you going to do about those?

→ Imagine yourself with total confidence in this theme. Write out what your service to others would look like and two things you could do to grow in this area.

→ If you are already secure in this theme, how would you begin to reproduce it in others?

Our strength as powerful caregivers comes from what we believe about God and ourselves. Do you think you have real life to give to others? Having confidence in yourself and your God emboldens you to continue to step into other people's lives with the hope that you offer. The more lives you enter; the more hope you will bring. I pray that this book and this paper help you on the path of unshakeable faith in yourself as a powerful caregiver.

This is a required step for those seeking certification from this academy. If you working through this paper for your own growth, you are still welcome to submit your work. It is encouraging to read others thoughts on this topic.

All papers can be emailed to **APC@josiahscovenant.com**.

We pray that this paper will tap you more into the love of God for all that you do and that this love may overflow onto everyone you come in contact with.

Blessings.

About the Author

Kevin Shorter is a writer and teacher with the focus on leading himself and others into the heart of God the Father. You can join the more than 20,000 that follow him on either his blog, prayer- coach.com, Twitter @Prayer_Coach or Facebook at PrayerCoachBlog.

Kevin and his wife, Allison, started the non-profit, Josiah's Covenant, which aims to create families for Asian orphans, provide them with job opportunities, teach them life skills, and keep them from being caught in the sex trade. They currently live in China with their two daughters. Find out more at JosiahsCovenant.com.

Other Books by the Author

Breaking Free: How to Be Completely Free From Any Addiction
- This book helps reduce the journey to freedom by:
  1. Reminding you of God's heart for your life.
  2. Identifying the roots of addiction.
  3. Finding tactics to remove the addiction.
  4. Seeing addiction from God's perspective.

2,500+ Prayer Quotes: Inspiration to Draw You Closer to God

- The desire of this book is to gather nuggets of wisdom from people who have spent time with God and journaled their findings. These quotes are intended to inspire us to continue our journey and fan the flame of passion to spend time with God.

Creative Intercession: How Simplicity, Fun, and Art Can Move the Hand of God

- Partnering with God doesn't have to be burdensome or make you weary. Come take a new adventure with Jesus and learn how to use everyday things like cooking, working, and hobbies to intercede for others. You will add power to your life and in the process enjoy a fun God!

One Last Thing...

If you enjoyed this book, please consider writing a review or sharing it with your friends. This would be greatly appreciated. Thanks.

Endnotes

[1] There is a generic stat that every 2.2 seconds an orphan ages out of the orphanage system. Some suggest this comes from UNICEF, but I haven't found proof. At best this can only be an approximation due to number of state-run and private systems all over the world.

[2] Reliable statistics are hard to find. This is often attributed to a Russian study, but the actual study is not given. Most sites just give the statistic without reference.

[1] Dekker, Ted. *Waking Up: To Who You Really Are (If You Dare)*. Outlaw Studios, 2015.

[2] Frankl, Viktor. "Youth in Search For Meaning." Viktor Frankl Institut, 1972. http://logotherapy.univie.ac.at/e/clipgallery.html.

[3] Jim. "How to Heal Families of Those Struggling With Alcohol Addiction." Seminar in Kunming, China, 28 Aug. 2016.

[4] Shorter, Kevin. *Breaking Free: How to Be Completely Free From Any Addiction*. 2014.

[5] Smith, E.E. "10 Careers With High Rates of Depression." *Psychology Today*, 24 Nov. 2010. www.psychologytoday.com/blog/not-born-yesterday/201011/ten-careers-high-rates-depression.

[6] Krejcir, Dr. Richard J. "Statistics on Pastors." Church Leadership, 2007. http://www.churchleadership.org/apps/articles/default.asp?articleid=42347&columnid=4545.

[7] Schaeffer Institute of Church Leadership Development 2007 study.

[8] "What is Caregiver Burnout?" *WebMD*, www.webmd.com/women/caregiver-recognizing-burnout#1. Accessed 8 Nov. 2016.

[9] Fink, Jennifer L.W. "5 Signs of Burnout." *NursingLink*, 16 May 2011. nursinglink.monster.com/benefits/articles/2481-5-signs-of-burnout.

[10] Krejcir, Dr. Richard J. "Statistics on Pastors." Church Leadership, 2007. http://www.churchleadership.org/apps/articles/default.asp?articleid=42347&columnid=4545.

[11] Krejcir, Dr. Richard J. "Statistics on Pastors." Church Leadership, 2007. http://www.churchleadership.org/apps/articles/default.asp?articleid=42347&columnid=4545.

9 780998 104522